IIS
7/09

DELTA TEACHER DEVELOPMENT SERIES

Series editors Mike Burghall and Lindsay Clandfield

# The Developing Teacher

## Practical activities for professional development

Duncan Foord

DELTA PUBLISHING

Published by
DELTA PUBLISHING
Quince Cottage
Hoe Lane
Peaslake
Surrey GU5 9SW
England

www.deltapublishing.co.uk

© Delta Publishing 2009

First published 2009

ISBN 978-1-905085-22-4

Edited by Mike Burghall
Designed by Christine Cox
Cover photo © iStockphoto.com/Nikada
Printed by Halstan & Co., Amersham, Bucks, England

## Acknowledgement

I would like to thank Nicola, and editors Lindsay and Mike,
for their fantastic feedback, support and encouragement;
Christine Cox, for designing a book so pleasing on the
eye and easy to follow; also the trainee teachers and
staff at OxfordTEFL Barcelona, for their comments and
contributions to my research on teacher development.

# From the author

I've been walking in the field of English Language Teaching for more than 20 years now.

My first job was teaching mixed-nationality groups in a language school in central London. I don't think I had much idea what I was doing or where I was going. I offered a pork pie to a Muslim student in a class on food vocabulary, and put my hand through a paper wall in a Japanese restaurant where I had been invited to join my students for supper. But it wasn't all bad. I dressed up as one of Cinderella's ugly sisters in a Christmas pantomime, and that seemed to go down well, especially when one of my balloons burst.

Later, things got a little more serious. I studied for an RSA DipTEFLA, a practical advanced qualification for language teachers (now known as the DELTA) and later did a Masters in ELT, continued teaching, worked as a director of studies, trained teachers, and opened a language and teacher-training school in Barcelona, where I am now. I train teachers and run the business. I also work as a moderator for Trinity College London CertTESOL courses, and write. Perhaps it's about time I did another pantomime?

That's my story, then.

ELT is very diverse and I've met lots of teachers, at different stages in their teaching careers, with different stories. Eduardo, Elena and Jack are made-up examples who represent differing personalities and differing attitudes to the profession, but all three of them would benefit from a thoughtful analysis of their current work situation and a commitment to their further development.

**Eduardo** has had a stable job for the last ten years, working for a good institution. He doesn't want to risk losing it. He is required to attend in-house workshops regularly, some of which he finds useful. He engages with colleagues in discussions about school policy on areas such as assessment and the syllabus. He considers himself a reflective teacher, and is quite critical of his own teaching. He cares a lot about his students and job satisfaction, and occasionally suffers from stress.

**Elena** has just completed her first term as a teacher of English at her local state school in Slovenia. She teaches secondary-age children. The first year is proving to be tough, but she is enjoying it and gaining confidence. It can be difficult to get the students to speak English in class and she

feels the syllabus is a bit of a constraint, with its emphasis on grammar, but she is excited about next year and trying out some new ideas she has. A scholarship is available to attend a short teacher-development course in the summer, and she is wondering whether to apply.

**Jack** has taught in six different countries for periods ranging from three months to two years. He has worked with all age groups and taught business English to adults. He likes to take on new challenges and believes he learns through experience. He focuses on earning enough to finance his travels. He becomes friends with some of his students, but doesn't spend too much time thinking about his classes or his students' learning. He gets on well with his colleagues but tends to be a professional loner and rarely participates in developmental activities.

When I look back over the years, I think there's something of me in all three of these teachers.

I wanted to write a book for teachers with 30 *days'* experience and 30 *years'* experience: for teachers as diverse in their situations and attitudes as Eduardo, Elena and Jack.

*The Developing Teacher* is a book, but it is a book of 'activity', so the main aim isn't reading, it is *doing*. Doing things on your own, with your students, with your colleagues and with your school; things which are interesting and fun, and which help you to understand your teaching better. In other words, multiple activities that have an impact on you and the people who work with you.

Another reason I wrote this book was for my own development. The process of writing things down, shaping and organising my ideas, and getting feedback from colleagues and editors, has helped me learn more about myself, about writing, about teaching and about teacher development.

So let's keep walking. Developing. We're all bound to get somewhere. Step by step.

Duncan

# Contents

| | |
|---|---|
| **Alice** | Would you tell me, please, which way I ought to go from here? |
| **Cheshire Cat** | That depends a good deal on where you want to get to. |
| **Alice** | I don't much care where ... |
| **Cheshire Cat** | Then it doesn't matter which way you go. |
| **Alice** | ... so long as I get *somewhere*. |
| **Cheshire Cat** | Oh, you're sure to do that, if you only walk long enough. |

*Alice's Adventures in Wonderland*, Lewis Carroll

## The developing teacher

It isn't the same thing having ten years' experience as having one year's experience repeated ten times.

This assertion, which is usually received with nods of agreement in discussions about teacher development, has two implications. Firstly, that development isn't possible without explicit and conscious changes in routine and activity. Secondly, that there are some teachers who do this and some who don't – they just repeat tried and tested routines year after year. In reality, teacher development is more complex and subtle. Development *can* happen naturally as a result of teachers going about their everyday business, and the dichotomy of developing and non-developing teachers is not helpful. We are all developing, the question is *how*.

**Teachers are all developing, the question is how.**

If we reflect on *where* we actually want to go, as opposed to simply 'getting somewhere', like Alice, and if we consider the action we can take to get there, we might find ourselves enjoying the sensation of walking quickly and confidently up an escalator, rather than laboriously up the stairs.

Let us begin to examine the nature of development by looking at some definitions of the word itself. Here are three definitions of 'development' from the *Collins Cobuild Dictionary*:

- The gradual growth or formation of something.
- The process or result of making a basic design gradually better and more advanced.
- An event or incident which has recently happened and is likely to have an effect on the present situation.

We should also bear in mind that 'develop' can be used as an intransitive or transitive verb: it can happen or it can be made to happen.

- 'I am developing.'
- 'I am developing myself.'
- 'I am developing a new approach to teaching pronunciation.'
- 'What can I do to develop my teachers?'

All the authors and experts quoted in *The Developing Teacher* are referenced in the Bibliography on page 18.

Let us begin, then, by addressing our three definitions. All three are relevant to an understanding of how development works and how the term is used in English Language Teaching.

### 'The gradual growth or formation of something'

In this definition, development is seen intransitively as something that happens over time: 'I am developing'. Teachers themselves naturally grow and develop as they gain experience teaching. As Alison Perkins says: *'If we are doing something we enjoy, then Continuous Professional Development is a natural component of our daily work life. It is an attitude.'*

Development is something gradual and inevitable.

Development is, therefore, something gradual and inevitable. Your growth may be influenced by your own conscious efforts, those of the school where you work, or it may happen naturally, so to speak, as a result of doing your job as a teacher. You can make things happen and you can react to things which happen to you at work. Events and circumstances such as a change of job, a new government policy, your staffroom colleagues or having a baby will shape the way you change as a teacher, as well as the decisions you make about how to teach your students better, what courses to attend and what books to read.

### 'The process or result of making a basic design gradually better and more advanced'

In this second definition, 'develop' is used transitively: 'I can develop myself or I can develop someone else'. There is a conscious effort to improve something. Development, or 'making better', can refer to efforts by individual teachers to improve themselves or by schools and institutions to promote teacher improvement. Training organisations offer 'teacher development courses' and schools often talk of their 'teacher development programmes'. Julian Edge (2002) has said: *'Training is what other people do to you. Development is what you do to yourself.'*

The distinction between *training* and *development* is blurred.

In ELT, however, the distinction is not always clear. Training courses and efforts by institutions to improve teaching often take a form which we might call 'supervised self-development'. Edge himself has also talked of 'cooperative development' to describe the way teachers can help each other to develop: *'I need someone to work with, but I don't need someone who wants to change me and make me more like the way they think I ought to be. I need someone who will help me see myself clearly.'* (1992)

### 'An event or incident which has recently happened and is likely to have an effect on the present situation'

In this definition, 'development' is a noun and refers to something that happens, rather than something you choose. Here are some examples of possible developments at your work:

- *Janet has decided to leave her post. Would you like to apply?*
- *We are installing interactive whiteboards in all the classrooms.*
- *Mishka's parents would like to speak to you about her progress. They aren't happy.*

'Development' can also be a countable or uncountable noun. The above are examples of developments (countable); things which happen that affect your work. Your reactions to these *developments* will shape your *development*. Will you apply for the new job? How will you use the new technology available? What will the parents say to you and how will that affect you (and your student)?

We have looked at three definitions of development and applied them to ELT. The conclusion would seem to be that you can change or develop in three ways:

- You change without noticing you have changed.
- You change by making things happen.
- You change as a result of things that happen to you.

Reactions to developments will shape your development.

Developmental 'activity', therefore, would aspire to capture all three of these dimensions, through multiple 'activities' that help you reflect on what has happened, that make new things happen and that help you react to change around you, as it happens.

But what kind of development are we talking about? The terms 'professional development' and 'teacher development' are often used interchangeably. *Teacher development* in some cases might refer to becoming better at what we do in the classroom. *Professional development* can refer to how we develop our career in teaching in the broadest sense, incorporating ambitions for promotion or recognition. Continuing *Professional* Development (CPD) is a term often used to describe structured schemes for development. The IATEFL Special

Interest Group (SIG) is for *Teacher* Development.

Clandfield and Kerr and Perkins have pointed out the problematic nature of the terms *profession* and *professional* in the context of teaching in general and ELT in particular. Given its diversity, can ELT be considered a profession? A career state school teacher in Slovenia and a young American TEFL teacher 'travelling and experiencing new cultures for a few years' may not have a great deal in common in terms of how they qualified, the type of teaching they do or the organisations to whom they are answerable.

# Why do we need teacher development?

Whether you consider yourself as part of a profession or not may influence the choices you make about your development, but the basic desire to 'do the best you can' for yourself and your students is shared by all teachers.

However, some teachers do have reservations about teacher development. Here is what 'Sam', a colleague, had to say:

*'I spend so much time just keeping up that I haven't developed as a teacher as I otherwise might have. You work so hard just to stay afloat, that attending workshops and development programmes or reading books is the last thing on your mind when you have free time. You want to get away from work ... not do more!'*

We can sympathise with Sam. Perhaps he's right. Dealing with all the challenges in a day's work is enough development for anyone. Prioritising your personal life can lead to you being a more rounded, happy person and a more interesting and positive presence and model for your students. Sam's weekend windsurfing is more likely to interest his teenage students than a Saturday workshop on interactive listening. Susan Barduhn has said that *'feeling good about yourself is your top professional responsibility'*.

On the other hand, the workshop could help Sam and his students to get the most out of his windsurfing anecdotes in class. Becoming a better teacher and enjoying life are not mutually exclusive, but there's a lot to fit in!

Sam could have covered the developmental ground of that Saturday workshop by thinking about his own teaching carefully *during the week*. He may have been puzzled or disappointed with his students' reactions to listening activities in class and, having jotted down some ideas on the bus home, decided to try something new.

Our question, then, can be better phrased. Rather than ask 'Why do we need teacher development?', let us assume that development is a given. If our definition takes in all three interpretations of development, as discussed, everyone will sign up for it, including Sam. Instead, then, we can frame the question like this: 'What are the different ways to develop?'

To address this, we need to look at how teachers learn, but before doing so, we can usefully examine another question frequently asked about teacher development.

# Who is responsible for teacher development?

If development is 'something you do to yourself', as Julian Edge suggests, then it makes sense to place responsibility with teachers themselves. Here are five reasons for taking the 'Do it yourself' approach:

- It favours 'bottom-up' approaches to learning. If teachers take charge of their development, either individually or collectively, it is likely to reflect their own needs and interests.
- If teachers initiate their developmental activity themselves, they are likely to feel more ownership of the process and follow through with it.
- Many teachers are freelance workers. They are not associated with a school, or work at more than one school.

- Teachers nowadays are likely to change schools more frequently in their career than in the past. As a teacher, you will increasingly be defined by who you are, not who you work for. Your career will include close and important connections with organisations, but its defining thread is you and what you have done.
- Some schools do very little, if anything, to promote teacher development, or when they do make efforts, they may not be appropriate. Teachers will need to take charge, if they want to make sure they move forward.

**Support from your school**

This is not to say that schools, universities and training companies cannot make an important contribution. In fact, they would be wise to do so, for three reasons:

- Facilitating development successfully will improve the effectiveness of their teachers.
- Good teachers will be attracted to the school, if they see it as a good place to develop, and this will in turn reduce staff turnover.
- If schools acknowledge and foreground their teachers as learners, then they will be modelling a learning culture to their students, which is likely to impact positively on their attitude to learning.

Here are the thoughts of a colleague, 'Petra':

*'Without support, I find teachers tend to respect the job less and may leave the field altogether. They may not realize the importance or need to further their development without the active involvement and encouragement of the institution. Additionally, many teachers lack the resources to further their development independently. My own development has been largely due to the schools that supported me most in taking further steps forward.'*

As a teacher, it can be unrealistic to depend on the organisation you work for to help your development. And it is also feasible to develop as a teacher in the most unpromising environments. In fact, sometimes, the more unpromising the environment the more robust the development! It is certainly not useful to shelve or compromise your own growth by waiting, making excuses or blaming others.

Let us suggest, therefore, that an effective approach is to start with developmental activity you can do yourself and then gradually expand your circle to include your students, your colleagues, your school and your profession. Bringing about change in institutions is your ultimate and most challenging act of development.

# How do teachers develop?

According to Freeman's descriptive model of the components of teaching there are four areas teachers can develop:

**Four areas to develop and seven ways to learn**

- *Skills* – You learn to do something, for example to give instructions more clearly.
- *Knowledge* – You learn about something, for example how the sounds of English are produced.
- *Awareness* – You learn how to use your eyes and ears better to find out what happens when you teach.
- *Attitude* – You learn about your assumptions about teaching, learning, yourself, your learners, your culture.

Your own development as a teacher is about how you grow and change in all of these four areas. So let us look at seven different ways this might occur.

### The blank slate or deficit model

*'Never having taught before, I am amazed at how much was covered in just one month.'* (Andrea)

Early models of teacher learning originating in the 60s and 70s were, not surprisingly, influenced by the behaviourist learning theories of the time. Becoming a teacher involved starting from scratch, a blank slate, and being trained in the appropriate skills and knowledge by experts.

To some extent, the idea still prevails in initial training courses, like the CELTA or Trinity CertTESOL courses, as referred to above by Andrea, a newly-qualified teacher, on completing her four-week initial training course. A teacher trainer once said, back in the mid-eighties, that the younger the trainees, ie the blanker the slate, the better teachers they made. Older trainees were more difficult to train because they came with baggage, experience and ideas which had to be erased.

Teacher learning was identified with further training, formal attempts to improve skills and instil better habits in teachers. This has also been referred to as a 'deficit model'. The teacher is seen as in some way lacking in relation to an ideal. Non-native teachers had a language deficit compared to natives, beginner teachers were deficient in terms of language awareness and appropriate methods and techniques compared to experienced teachers.

The problem with the blank slate or deficit model is neatly summarised by Marland:

*'The explanations given by teachers for what they do are typically not derived from what they were taught in teacher education programs … Rather, the classroom actions of teachers are guided by internal frames of reference which are deeply rooted in personal experiences, especially in-school ones, and are based on interpretations of those experiences.'*

### The science model
*'I enjoy knowing more and more about the world of TEFL and the English language and being able to employ this knowledge in the classroom.'* (Carla)

Zahorik suggests three conceptions of how teaching is learnt: science-research, theory-philosophy and art-craft.

The science-research model says that teachers learn by following methods that research has proved or suggested is effective. The Audio-Lingual Approach or Neuro-Linguistic Programming (NLP) might fall into this category. If you are a teacher who learns in this way, you are likely to take an interest in published research and studies, or at least note reference to them in more general books on methodology. You will seek evidence beyond your own experience and intuition to help you decide what is best in the classroom. For example, you read that several studies have shown that the third person 's' tends to be acquired late by second language learners, so you decide to stop correcting your students when they make mistakes such as *'my sister go …'.*

### The theory-philosophy model
*'Taking the Trinity Diploma in TESOL also contributed greatly to my teacher development. I felt that I had reached a stage in my career where I needed to have a greater understanding of the ideas and theory behind EFL and a chance to put these ideas into practice.'* (Jane)

The theory-philosophy conception says that teachers are guided by what should or ought to work, in other words by moral or political values. Communicative and humanistic approaches would fall into this category. The idea that languages are best learned if the learning is student-centred, with the teacher as a facilitator, has developed hand-in-hand with trends towards individual choice and rejections of authoritarian political models in the late 20th century western democracies. If you are a teacher who learns this way, you are likely to fit your teaching to ideas and principles rather than hard facts and will take less note of the results of studies than of ideas. You prefer *approaches* to *methods*.

### The art-craft model
*'Time in the classroom. Time with the students you teach. Building a rapport and understanding. Experience develops you. What works and what doesn't, and most importantly, what works with who. Know your audience!'* (Magda)

The art-craft model emphasises that teaching is invention and personalisation. The metaphor suggests that teachers *'acquire a personal repertoire of specialised skills and techniques and that these may be unique to each teacher and hence in some sense unpredictable'* (Richards). It also implies that learning might take place through observation and contact with a 'master craftsman', or mentor, rather than formal training. If you are an art-craft teacher, you will concentrate on developing your experience and know-how. You like to improvise and accept an element of mystery in learning and teaching. You make decisions based on intuition, what *seems* to work rather than what *should* work or what is *proved* to work.

## Reflective teaching

*'As often as not, some great new idea quite thoroughly bombs in the classroom for whatever reason. It is important to me to use this as crucial evidence of my development. I need to reflect and ask: Why didn't it work? What could I do differently next time? Would this work better with a different group?'* (Simon)

Cruickshank and Applegate define reflective teaching as *'the teacher thinking about what happens in classroom lessons and thinking about alternative means of achieving goals or aims'.* (cited in Bartlett)

Bartlett himself widens the definition to include a social dimension: *'Becoming a reflective teacher is intended to allow us to develop ourselves individually and collectively, to deal with contemporary events and structures and not to take these structures for granted'.* (Bartlett)

Donald Schon distinguishes between reflection-on-action and reflection-in-action. The former refers to critical analysis by teachers *before and after* teaching, the latter to the reflections teachers make *while* teaching.

You can reflect alone or with a colleague about your teaching. Reflection can be brief thoughts and discussion or a long-term activity, such as keeping a teaching journal or collating reflections over a period of time. Long-term reflection on action can also incorporate reading and attention to theory. The reflective model of how teachers learn emphasises learning using classroom teaching as the starting point and analysing outcomes critically. This may seem like common sense. After all, reflecting on what we do is standard human behaviour in a range of contexts. Common sense, though, isn't always common practice. The traditional transmission model of learning, derived from the blank slate idea, leads teachers to look for authority from experts and researchers, rather than from themselves and their own teaching. The reflective model is empowering in the sense that it hands authority to teachers. You are in charge of your own learning.

## Teacher learning as personal construction

*'When a group of teachers gather together to discuss their own development and ideas about teaching, the exchange of ideas and sharing of knowledge empowers everyone concerned. The pooled experience that we have as a group of teachers is enormous, and we all have something to learn from each other.'* (Jonathan)

Adults don't learn in the same way as children and most teachers are adults. Richards and Farrell, Roberts, and Mohamed, among others, have highlighted the importance of *constructivism*, the idea that, especially in the case of adults, knowledge is actively constructed by learners, not passively received. This is the opposite of the blank slate idea. The slate isn't blank at all – it has already been written on. In this model, activities such as self-monitoring, reflecting on experience and journal writing are particularly appropriate for development, as they help learners fit new learning into their personal framework.

In a constructivist approach to teacher observation, for example, the observer will encourage the teacher being observed to set their own developmental agenda. Rather than say *'you could improve on this'*, the observer will say *'what do you think you should improve on?'* and resist any temptation to influence the response. Change happens for adults when they are ready and willing. It might be objected that this is like asking someone to comb their hair without a mirror. Adults want to know how others see them, as well as how they see themselves. In fact, the two are connected. A middle way in the above example might be for the observee to elicit selected judgemental comments from the observer.

### Using role models

*'You learn from people with more experience than you. Not necessarily your bosses but people you can look up to. I guess that means experience again! Learn from your elders and those wiser than you.'* (Karina)

Learning from an inspirational example

The idea that teachers can learn from imitating expert practitioners is not new (see the art-craft model above). According to Allwright and Bailey, classroom research is *'all about gaining a better understanding of what good teachers (and learners) do instinctively as a matter of course, so that ultimately all can benefit'.* Use of role models has been supported more recently by theories derived from NLP, which advocate reference to models of excellence in learning. Mentoring and teacher observation can be used for this purpose.

If the role model becomes a guru, there is always a danger that the uncritical follower will fail to develop their own unique teaching style and possibly seek to imitate undesirable aspects of their teaching, or aspects that work for the guru but not the follower.

# What stops teachers developing?

Having looked at the way teachers *can* and *do* learn, let us now consider some constraints, some of the obstacles that *prevent* teachers from learning.

### Attitudes

John Dewey lists three key attitudes as necessary for teachers: open-mindedness, responsibility and whole-heartedness. A teacher with these attitudes is likely to succeed in developing effectively. The opposites to Dewey's three attitudes are fear of change, a tendency to blame others and laziness. Of course, teachers are not either one or the other, but we can examine ourselves in terms of these opposites and plot ourselves at a point on a line somewhere between the two. Our attitudes are not fixed – they vary according to what activities we are engaged in and when – but the aggregate over the years will determine our development.

### Colleagues

Colleagues are a potential source of strength, confidence and inspiration, a positive support in our development as teachers. They can also be a negative influence. Joachim Appel has used the term 'community of moaners' to describe himself and his staffroom colleagues. *'Staffroom talk is brimming over with anger and aggression. It is a release of tension. It is irrational and it accentuates the negative … shared suffering is easily mistaken for a set of shared values, which of course does not exist.'.* Does this sound like a description of the staffroom where you work? A dash of realism and dark humour can have a positive effect, and is probably essential to some degree, especially in very challenging teaching contexts. But entrenched cynicism, particularly if it comes from senior staff, can serve to curb the enthusiasm and motivation of others to take what they do seriously.

Individual and collective obstacles to development

### Stress

Maslach used the term 'burnout' to describe the job stress often experienced among individuals who do jobs which involve a lot of personal contact with people, such as teachers, nurses and social workers: *'Burnout is a syndrome of emotional exhaustion, depersonalisation and reduced personal accomplishment'.*

Teacher development can be a means of combating burnout, otherwise the burnout can cramp the development.

### Schools

Teachers' reservations about teacher development are not necessarily the result of resistance to change itself, but may reflect distaste for the organised 'top-down' versions of development sometimes promoted in schools. Not everyone enjoys doing a Mexican wave at the match. Some people just want to watch the game. Well-intentioned schemes may actually discourage development if they are poorly managed. Equally, a lack of attention to teacher development in a school can seriously discourage teachers.

You, your colleagues and your school can all help and hinder your development. It can cut both ways.

# Five circles of development

So how can you approach teacher development in practical terms? In order to understand and talk about teacher development more easily, we can propose a model which organises developmental activity into five categories. These can be represented in five concentric circles.

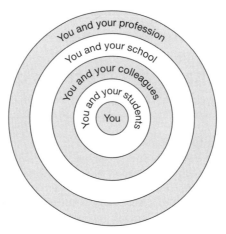

- The first circle, the inner circle, involves 'you', the teacher, working alone. Reading this book or reflecting on a class you have taught would be examples of such individual activity.
- The second circle is 'you and your students'. Development in this circle would include getting feedback from students about your teaching or trying out new material with them.
- The third circle is 'you and your colleagues'. Activity here might include peer observation, team teaching and staffroom support.
- The fourth circle, 'you and your school', includes teachers' meetings, carrying out projects, and interaction with management and other members of staff.
- The fifth circle is 'you and your profession'. Examples would be attending and presenting at conferences, membership of professional communities, and writing for publication.

These circles are useful for two reasons:

**The 'five circles' model reflects both diversity and challenge.**

### They cater for the diversity in ELT

As we have observed, teaching English is a very diverse profession. Some teachers work in relative isolation as freelance teachers and will find it useful to have activities grouped together which don't involve colleagues or institutions. And teachers have different preferred development styles: some will prefer to emphasise individual work, others will tend to collaboration.

### They reflect the challenges of development

They represent a natural progression in teacher development in the sense that activities tend to get more difficult the further we go from the centre. Working with colleagues and our school or profession presents challenges of leadership and co-operation.

Stephen Covey proposes a three-tier model for personal development, which mirrors our growth as human beings from *dependence* to *independence* and finally to *interdependence*. According to his model, independence is a pre-requisite for interdependence. Applying this to teaching, we can say that it is when we are confident and autonomous teachers that we can most usefully contribute to bringing about change with our colleagues, in our school and in our profession.

Flight attendants like to remind us to fit our own oxygen mask before attempting to help others fit theirs. As teachers, it makes sense to feel comfortable and confident in ourselves and our classroom before attempting to engage with others. However, attention to each circle will, of course, never be strictly chronological.

# Steps to development

It can be helpful to think of development as having two potential 'sources':

- The kind we seek out (teacher as hunter).
- The kind that is thrust upon us (teacher as hunted).

Development is both pro-active and re-active.

Attending a local conference or experimenting with new material are matters of choice. A formal observation and appraisal from our director of studies, or an interview with a dissatisfied parent, are not. We are hunters and hunted and both types of scenario are likely to influence our professional development.

It is important to cover both these sources of development. Some require you to hunt; others require you to reflect on being hunted. In either case, the steps you take will have varying impact on your development. It is difficult to generalise about what kind of activity or event will have the greatest impact, as this will probably depend on the individual teacher. Another metaphor for this might be that of a dance: the result of the interplay between the pro-active and re-active elements of development, where leading and following are both key elements in achieving smooth and harmonious movement.

The development continuum illustrated below is based on research from the world of business and represents what might be seen as the likely impact of steps we take in our development as teachers.

**Developmental impact**

| Less ← | | | | → More |
|---|---|---|---|---|
| Training Workshops Reading | Assessed training Role modelling | Feedback/ coaching | Development in job | Job change |
| Knowledge transfer Professional setting | Copying a skill or behaviour | Coaching Boss/mentor relationship | Projects Responsibility Accountability | |
| Education-based | Education/ Relationship-based | Relationship-based | Experience-based | |

The table suggests that experience-based development is likely to have more impact than education-based development, particularly when the education is not combined with formal assessment and does not build significant relationships. This is not to devalue education. A mix of education-based, relationship-based and experience-based activity is probably the best way to maximise development. Formally assessed professional qualifications, such as the Trinity Diploma in TESOL or the Cambridge DELTA, incorporate relationship-based elements, such as mentoring, and experience-based elements, such as supervised research,

Education versus on-the-job experience

which go beyond knowledge transfer models of learning. This type of course is likely to stimulate a richer developmental experience.

There will be moments in your teaching career when taking a course or working towards a professional qualification is a very positive step, which will stimulate tremendous achievement.

However, the table also suggests that the jobs you do during your career will provide the most powerful influence on your development. This shouldn't be a surprise. Developing through responsibility and accountability in your job is the equivalent of your learners improving their English by having real conversations with English speakers, taking responsibility for successful communication. Just as good teachers integrate real conversations into the classroom to help their students develop their English, the developing teacher will incorporate a developmental twist into their work to help their own development. We could say that development, in this sense, isn't so much about *activity* as about *attitude*.

**Matching activity and attitude, challenge and skill**

So how does this attitude look or feel? Csikszentmihalyi has defined 'flow', or 'satisfaction', as an optimum state of affairs where challenge and skill are matched. Low challenge combined with high skill leads to frustration and boredom ('flight'), and high challenge with low skill to anxiety ('fight'). We can adopt this idea to create what might be called 'developmental flow', represented in the following diagram (adapted).

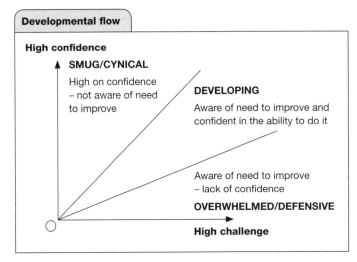

The aim, of course, is to spend as much time as possible in the middle section, 'Developing', and to be aware that when we are outside this sector, we need to either boost our confidence or give ourselves a challenge to get back there.

# Stepping forward

We have taken a very brief overview of some of the key theories and models of teacher learning to emerge in the last 50 years. The tendency has been to move away from a transmission-style model of learning to favour a more experience-based approach. Formal professional qualifications have themselves developed to incorporate more reflective and classroom-based activity and less knowledge transmission, to the extent that 'training' in this context has become what we might call 'supervised development'.

However, it is worth remembering that teachers (like language learners) learn in different ways and can benefit from a variety of experiences. There is no right and wrong way to develop. The teachers quoted in these pages support different and even contradictory ideas about how we learn. Questioned on the three most important events in their development, answers included mention of role models, reading, teaching experiences, training courses, their next door neighbour, in fact all the above ideas and theories of how teachers learn were represented.

An activity-based approach

As its title suggests, *The Developing Teacher* takes an activity-based approach to teacher development. The different ways of teacher learning we have outlined are reflected, but in each case the ideas and theories are framed and carried forward in a step-by-step activity. The activities themselves are underpinned by four key principles.

### Developing by doing

You do things and learn from the experience. This is not to say that reading and understanding theory is not a good idea. Reading and reflecting on theory can be a powerful tool for development. As Michael Lewis once said, there is nothing more practical than a good theory. Reflection without action, though, is like making a shopping list when you have no money or trolley. In *The Developing Teacher*, development is approached in terms of impact, as well as awareness.

### Making things happen

Four ways to keep developing successfully

For teacher development to really work for you, you may need some help in making sure you are organised and can prioritise. Reading that new methodology book is the easy part. The hard bit is actually making time to sit down with it in the first place. You need to address time management, leadership, personal organisation and motivation to help you make things happen.

### Making the most of things that happen to you

Bearing in mind things will happen which you haven't planned or aimed for, it is also important to think about how to make the most of situations as they arise and exploit them to your benefit or at least limit negative effects. When you can't make the most of a situation, you need to make the *best* of it.

### Linking teacher development to self-development

Your students respond to *who you are* as well as *what you do* in the classroom, so keeping a sense of balance between work and other parts of your life will have a positive impact on your teaching.

To conclude, a personal anecdote: I once interviewed a teacher for a job and asked her why she thought she would be suitable for the post. 'Well', she said, 'I am a happy, positive person.' That certainly wasn't the answer I was expecting and of course, there is much more to being a good teacher, but that, I thought, is a very good place to start!

# Bibliography

Allwright, D and Bailey, K M *Focus on the Language Classroom: An introduction to classroom research for language teachers* CUP 1991

Appel, J *Diary of a Language Teacher* Heinemann ELT 1995

Bailey, K M, Curtis, A and Nunan, D *Pursuing Professional Development: The self as source* Thomson 2001

Barduhn, S 1999 In 'Continuing Professional Development – Some of our perspectives' Edge, J (Ed) IATEFL Publications 2002

Bartlett, L 'Teacher development through reflective teaching' In Richards, J C and Nunan, D (Eds) *Second Language Teacher Education* CUP 1990

Brown, J D and Wolfe-Quintero, K 'Teacher Portfolios for evaluation: A great idea or a waste of time?' *Language Teacher* 21(1) 1997

Clandfield, L and Kerr, P *Professionalism in ELT: An obscure object of desire* IATEFL Publications 2004

Covey, S *The Seven Habits of Highly Effective People* Franklin Covey Co 1989

Curran, C *Counseling-Learning in Second Languages* Apple River Press 1976

Csikszentmihalyi, M *Beyond Boredom and Anxiety* Jossey-Bass 1975

Dewey, J *How We Think* Henry Regnery 1933

Edge, J (Ed) *Continuing Professional Development – Some of our perspectives* IATEFL Publications 2002

Edge, J 'Co-operative Development' *ELT Journal* 46(1) 1992

Evans, S M *Professional Portfolios: Documenting and presenting performance excellence* Teachers' Little Secrets 1995

Fanselow, J *Breaking Rules* Pearson Education 1987

Freeman, D 'Teacher training, development and decision making: A model of teaching and related strategies for language teacher education' *TESOL Quarterly* 23(1) 1989

Heron, J *The Complete Facilitator's Handbook* Kogan-Page 2004

Herrmann N, Herrmann International website *www.hbdi.com*

Lewis, M *Implementing the Lexical Approach: Putting theory into practice* LTP 1997

Luft, J and Ingram, H *Of Human Interaction* National Press Books 1969

Malderez, A and Bodoczky, C *Mentor Courses: A resource book for trainer-trainers* CUP 1999

Marland, P W 'Implicit theories of teaching' In Anderson, L W (Ed) *International Encyclopaedia of Teaching and Teacher Education*, 2nd ed. Pergamon 1995

Maslach, C *Burnout: The cost of caring* Prentice Hall 1982

Mohamed, N 'Meaningful professional development' *English Teaching Professional* 42 2006

Perkins, A 1998 In 'Continuing Professional Development – Some of our perspectives' Edge, J (Ed) IATEFL Publications 2002

Richards, J C and Farrell, T S C *Professional Development for Language Teachers: Strategies for teacher learning* CUP 2005

Roberts, J *Language Teacher Education* Arnold 1998

Schon, D A *The Reflective Practitioner: How professionals think in action* Basic Books 1983

Sinclair, J et al *Collins Cobuild Advanced Learners English Dictionary* HarperCollins 2006

Zahorik, J A *Acquiring Teaching Skills* Journal of Teacher Education 21(5) 1986

***The Developing Teacher*** provides a bank of activities spread over five sections, our five circles. It is not intended that you work through the activities in the first circle in the order they appear. Nor that you work through the five circles in the book in order. Your development is exactly that: your development.

However, it is probably the case that as you move outwards, from circle to circle, the activities become more challenging, so if you are looking for a good place to start, then start with yourself, 'you'.

### Step-by-step development

Teachers are busy people. The activities are designed to require minimum time for you to do them. Many, in fact, simply add 'a developmental twist' to regular classroom practice, in the spirit of what Allwright and Bailey refer to as 'exploratory practice'.

Teachers are also well-accustomed to activities that have a clear step-by-step description, so the recognizable presentation of these activities will be familiar to you and this should make them easy to use.

- All the activities are preceded by a ***Rationale***. This describes briefly what the outcome of the activity is and why it can be useful for your development. The heading ***Activity*** tells you what exactly you will be doing.
- The procedures are clearly set out in a series of ***Steps***. These help you to break the activity down and carry it through to its conclusion. Of course, you may want to miss steps out, rearrange some of them or add your own: as with language teaching activities, all procedures can be adapted.

The activities can be done on their own, randomly, or compiled. You may wish to simply dip in and experiment, as and when you can, or you may save them for further reference and reflection in a portfolio.

### Organised development

You can, therefore, create your own 'teacher development course' by selecting, carrying out and saving the activities you choose. If you do this, you will probably find that the 'whole' of everything you achieve adds up to more than the sum of the various parts. The decision is yours.

Many of the activities include the use of a grid or Pro-forma to help direct and organise your planning and reflection. Space here does not permit full-size photocopiable Pro-formas. In many cases, you can make copies which you will find perfectly usable. In others, you can recreate the Pro-forma yourself from the model given, adapting it wherever necessary to your personal situation.

# You

The activities in the first circle can all be done independently, although you may find it useful to share them with others, if you have the opportunity. There are good reasons for considering the activities in this circle as your starting point, one of the most important being that interacting with students, colleagues and your school will require more planning and more interpersonal and leadership skills.

There are two further reasons (one practical and one pedagogical) why this circle might be of immediate interest.

- You work somewhere where you are the only teacher, or you are a freelance teacher who has little contact with other teachers.
- Your learning style is intra-personal. You prefer to do things on your own.

Opposite is a checklist of things you can do independently to develop yourself and your teaching. Which have you already done? Which of the things are of particular interest to you? Which have you not thought of doing? Which might you like to concentrate on? Read through the list and give yourself a score for each item.

The following brief introduction to the four sections of the first circle will help to contextualise the activities.

### Thinking about your development

First of all, it is crucial to understand your own situation and motivations; this in turn will help you prioritise your actions.

There are four basic *motivations for development*. These are summarised in the acronym RISE, which we shall be encountering again and again as we move from circle to circle. We engage in professional development with one (or a combination) of these motivations in mind.

- **R**ecognition: this can be sought from peers, colleagues, fellow professionals and students. Sharing your materials with colleagues and publishing an article are examples of this.
- **I**mposition: we engage in an activity because we have to. It is imposed by our boss, our school, our education authority or perhaps our students. A compulsory staff training day is a good example of this.
- **S**elf-improvement: we commit to activities in order to become better teachers. An example might be recording or videoing ourselves teaching.
- **E**njoyment: we engage in a professional development activity simply because it is enjoyable or fun.

---

**Personal checklist**

There are things you can do on your own to develop yourself and your teaching. Read down the list.

- Give yourself a score from 0-5 for each item, according to how often you do it (0 = 'never done this', 5 = 'done this a lot').
- Then complete the right-hand column, adding a tick (✔) where appropriate, if you would like to try something, or do more of it.

| Things I have done (or not done) ... | Score (0-5) | (✔) |
|---|---|---|
| Worked on my time management skills | | |
| Reflected on the best way for me to develop | | |
| Completed self-diagnostic tests to find out my learning style or personality type | | |
| Reflected on my own teaching | | |
| Learnt another language | | |
| Dealt with something stressing me | | |
| Read a professional journal | | |
| Read a book about TEFL | | |
| Kept a teaching diary | | |
| Created a teaching portfolio | | |
| Improved my English | | |
| Improved my knowledge of grammar/phonology | | |

**Comment**

Looking at this list should help identify areas of particular interest for you (or that you hadn't perhaps thought of before) and will help you decide which activities you would most like to do, or feel you most *need* to do!

---

Then there are two potential *sources of development*:

- The kind we seek out - the teacher as 'hunter'
- The kind thrust upon us - the teacher as 'hunted'

Attending a local conference, or experimenting with new material, are matters of choice. A formal observation and appraisal from our director of studies, or an interview with a dissatisfied parent, are not. Both types of scenario are likely to influence our professional development. An alternative to this metaphor, and one with a more human touch, is to think of development as a dance, where success and harmony arise from combining personal initiatives with an attentive response to the movements of others.

When making decisions about where to start 'hunting', or what moves to make on the dance floor, checklists like the one above can be helpful. An alternative is to take a particular difficulty or irritation at work as a starting point, and try to solve the problem. There is an activity to help you to do this.

## Organising yourself

The menu in the checklist is deliberately appealing: selecting things you would *like* to do is relatively easy. The hard part is making them *happen*. This involves allocating time and attention to activities and committing to seeing them through. There isn't much use in a shopping list if you don't then go to the shops!

The activities in this section will help you to go shopping. They help you become aware of what is involved in the action you have chosen and provide a step-by-step framework which will support and motivate you. The principles of personal organisation and time management are crucial to successful development.

## Getting to know yourself

There are three types of question teachers ask themselves.

- **Micro** questions concern the hundreds of small decisions we make each day, such as: How long will it take my students to finish the vocabulary exercise? How will I stop Ivan disrupting the class today?
- **Macro** questions deal with less frequent and bigger decisions about teaching: What coursebook will I use with this group? How could I motivate my class of teenagers better?
- **Meta** (meaning 'outside' or 'beyond') questions are even less frequent and even bigger: What kind of teacher am I? How did I become like this? *Why am I a teacher?*

The four activities in this section focus on meta questions. This is not to suggest that these questions are more important, quite the contrary in fact. They are, however, less frequently addressed in our day-to-day teaching and it seems worthwhile, therefore, to draw attention to them. There is, for example, a self-diagnostic learning style/personality test, which encourages you to discover your own typical style and preferences (and colour!) and to consider how these might impact on your teaching.

How we teach is determined not only by the experiences, training and development we undergo, but also the experiences, assumptions and values we form *before* we start teaching. Another way of getting to know ourselves is by reflecting on past and present role models. The activities *My favourite teacher* and *The Magnificent Seven* focus on this.

## Looking at yourself

Starting with a new class, a photocopier which doesn't work, dealing with school administration, a complaint from a parent, unsympathetic managers, writing reports, being observed, a sense of stagnation: these are some of the day-to-

day challenges teachers face. Many teachers devote so much attention to these challenges that they forget to take care of themselves! Looking after yourself (in mind, body and spirit) is central to your development as a teacher. If you are healthy and happy, you are more likely to be able to help your learners and achieve your personal goals. Remember what the flight attendants say when demonstrating the emergency procedures: always make sure you fit your own oxygen mask before helping others with theirs! In the activity *Tea and two biscuits*, you get a chance to think about how to manage stress.

There are also two activities in this section which get you to focus on your teaching through *self-observation*. This means you teach a class and make reflective notes, before, during and after the class, with the aim of understanding your teaching better. It is a good idea to:

- try to incorporate this kind of activity into your teaching routine. Set yourself a modest goal (one self-observation per month, for example);
- have a specific focus for the observation and reflection (think about a specific concern you have about your teaching or about a particular class);
- write things down to help the reflective process. You can make notes before, during or after the class, or a combination of all three;
- use a worksheet (or 'Pro-forma') to guide your notes and thoughts.

The advantage of self-observation is that it is non-threatening. You judge yourself. You are not obliged to disclose your reflections, though you may find it useful to share and talk through your notes with a colleague, if you feel comfortable doing so.

The last two activities focus on developing understanding of language and methodology. An important component of development for non-native teachers may be improving their knowledge of English, while many native-speaker teachers find it useful to understand more about how the language works, including the rules that underpin phonology, lexis and grammar. For all teachers, reversing roles and actually becoming a language student can be a very powerful tool, through experiencing what works (and doesn't work!) for you as a learner.

The activities in this circle help you to develop, through gaining a much clearer understanding of the kind of teacher you are and the challenges you face in your work. They also help to develop key personal organisation skills which you will be able to apply to the activities in the other circles.

The second circle activities will foster your development through engaging with your students, the people who perhaps stand most to gain from it!

# RISE and shine

### Four motivations for professional development

### Rationale
Understanding why you are interested in professional development will help you focus your efforts effectively.

### Activity
To reflect on your career as a teacher and your motivations.

---

### Step One
Read the story of Laura's career as a teacher, and notice her different motivations.

### Step Two
Look at the motivations behind engaging in professional development as summarised, using the acronym RISE, in the box below.

> **R**ecognition
> This can be in terms of job status, money or recognition from fellow professionals.
>
> **I**mposition
> Participation in a development scheme, or completing a formal qualification; it may be imposed by your employer or be something you feel obliged to undertake to be marketable; or making changes in your teaching as a result of feedback from a student or director of studies.
>
> **S**elf-improvement
> Development as a route to job satisfaction and a sense of self-worth. Improving your teaching knowledge and skills.
>
> **E**njoyment
> Development activity, such as travel and contact with fellow professionals, can be enjoyable for its own sake, without necessarily contributing to the above.

Read Laura's story again and label the different events with the letters R, I, S or E. Some will have a combinations of letters.

### Step Three
Assign events from your own career into the four categories using the Pro-forma opposite. You will, of course, find that some events fit more than one category. In this case, try to think of your primary motive. Do you notice any category predominating? Keep this document on file.

### Step Four
Return to the document in three months' time. Look back at your professional life over these three months. What has happened in each of the four categories? Add notes to your document. You should now have a clearer idea about the motivations that influence your own professional development. You may want to include this document at the start of a teaching portfolio (see Part C of *The Developing Teacher*).

---

**Laura's story**

*Laura graduated with a degree in Spanish and spent two years teaching in Colombia. She didn't have a teaching qualification and was obliged to learn about teaching on the job. Fortunately, she worked in a school where she found a lot of support from her colleagues. She improved her Spanish and enjoyed travelling around South America. Laura decided she wanted to return to Europe and as there was more competition for jobs there, she signed up for an intensive Certificate TESOL course in Barcelona. The course was tough but she really enjoyed it. After three years' teaching in Barcelona she decided to do a Diploma course, partly because she really enjoyed learning more about her job and partly because she wanted to work as a teacher trainer. She passed the course and worked as a teacher trainer. After two years, the school where Laura was working closed down. She decided to make a change, too. Feeling a little burnt out with training teachers on intensive courses, she decided to return to the classroom as a teacher of business English. Laura was very successful and her employers decided to promote her to the position of senior teacher.*

| RISE | |
|------|---|
| **R** | |
| **I** | |
| **S** | |
| **E** | |

# The hunter and the hunted

## Two sources of professional development

### Rationale
This activity helps you to reflect on how your development is a result of both pro-active and re-active measures you take. You seek out events (hunter) and respond to events which happen around you (hunted).

### Activity
To reflect on key moments in your career experience, become more aware of how they have affected you, and consider changing your strategy in future.

### Step One
Think about your career so far. Identify six (or more) key moments, events, activities or projects which have had a significant impact on you.

### Step Two
Note them down in the two columns. Were you hunter or hunted?

| Hunter | Hunted |
|---|---|
| Decided to move to a different school. | Observed by my director of studies. |
| | |

### Step Three
Consider the following questions:
- Which column has had the most influence on your teaching and your career?
- Are you happy with the balance you have?
- Think about one or more role models you have in your work or profession. What hunting have *they* done? How do *they* react to being hunted?

### Step Four
The first three steps of this activity have been reflective. Now looking forward, are you going to change anything about the way you approach your working life as a result this reflection? Do you think you need to do more (or less) hunting, or to react differently to situations where you are hunted? Can the two types of scenario be resolved harmoniously? Write down and keep what you propose to do, for future reference.

# D-I-Y development

## Planning a start on your development

### Rationale
One way to start thinking about your development is to ask yourself what you *don't* like about your work and plan some changes: some 'do it yourself' development.

### Activity
To think about some dissatisfactions with your working life and resolve to make changes.

### Step One
Look at the grid below. Make a list in the left-hand column of things you dislike about your job, inside and outside the classroom. Some examples are given for you.

| I don't like ... | Can I change it? (✔ ? X) |
|---|---|
| Spending so much time marking homework | |
| My long journey to work | |
| The coursebook for my upper-intermediate class | |
| My salary | |

### Step Two
Read through your list and for each item in the list decide if you can change it. Put a ✔, ? or X in the box beside it.
- ✔ Definitely can change
- ? Maybe can change
- X Definitely cannot change

### Step Three
Now look at the X items and think about them again. Be more optimistic. Change at least one of them to a ?.

### Step Four
Choose one of the ✔ or ? items and complete the chart below. Write the item and then write some notes on how you will make the change.

| I don't like: |
|---|
| How I will change this? |
| When? |
| How? |
| Who will be involved? |

### Step Five
You have created your own teacher development activity. Good luck with it. When you have done it, create another 'mini action plan' like this one. Keep going!

# First things first

## Deciding what matters most

### Rationale

One reason teachers give for not achieving developmental aims is 'lack of time'. This activity helps us to think about using the time we do have more effectively.

### Activity

To use the 'four quadrant' model to manage your time.

---

### Step One

Read the explanation of the four quadrant model opposite.

### Step Two

Look at the example of how a teacher might classify some weekly activities. Notice that these activities can appear in different quadrants. Some of the teacher's lesson and materials preparation is important, but some may be unnecessary or unimportant. The same goes for meetings.

### Step Three

Think about your last week at work. Write the different activities that occupied you in the four quadrants.

### Step Four

Make more time for Quadrant II activities. Look at the other three quadrants and do the following:

- Think of *one* activity you could move from QI to QII (to reduce last-minute-panic working).
- Think of *one* item from QIII and *one* from QIV which could be reduced or eliminated (to create more time).

### Step Five

During your working week, pause at random moments and ask yourself: *What quadrant am I in now?* Make some notes.

### Step Six

Repeat Step Three one week later. Use your field notes from Step Four to help you. Remember, your aim is to make QII grow and the other three quadrants shrink.

### Step Seven

Reflect: Are you making progress? Is Quadrant II growing? If not, try to look again at the other three quadrants, enlist the help of a friend or colleague if you can, and brainstorm ideas, and then try one more week!

The four quadrant model (adapted from Stephen Covey) has two axes, 'important' and 'urgent', which generate four quadrants, inside which we can classify the different activities we do in a week. To manage our time effectively, especially with professional development in mind, we need to maximise the time we spend in Quadrant II.

- Quadrant I activities are routine (teaching a class, meeting a parent, writing reports).
- Quadrant II activities involve planning and development (planning to use new material, reading, thinking, following a course).
- Quadrant III and IV activities are not important, but often occupy a lot of our time, especially the third quadrant, where apparent urgency can create a false impression of importance.

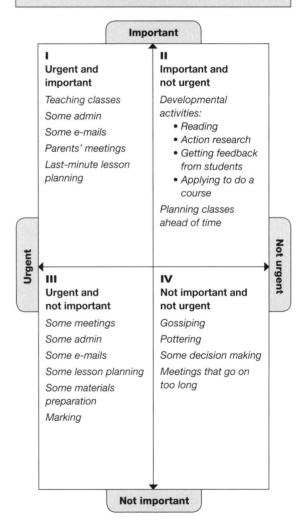

# Eight days a week

## Managing your time effectively

## Rationale

Some professional development activities require time outside class to carry out, so it is important to allocate this time if you want to make them happen. The key to time management is being committed to fulfilling your agenda.

## Activity

To plan time to carry out your developmental agenda and to stick to your plan.

## Step One

Buy a diary which shows a week on each double-page spread.

## Step Two

At the start of the week, or the end of the previous week, block your teaching hours and other commitments in the diary.

## Step Three

Do the following:

- Allocate an amount of time to your development activity (DA). For example, if you want to read a professional journal, allocate the time you need (say 30 minutes).
- Decide when you will do this and block the time into your weekly plan.
- Take note of the advice below.

### Managing times

| DO ... | DON'T ... |
|---|---|
| • plan weekly; <br> • use a diary and have it to hand; <br> • block in time to do things, as if they were a class. | • open your e-mails first thing in the morning; <br> • always say 'yes' to people; <br> • admit interruptions. |

## Step Four

**Either:**

Celebrate! You did what you planned. You managed your time.

**Or:**

Reflect and try again. You didn't do what you planned, or perhaps you succeeded only partially. Think about why, and make some notes using the following prompts.

### Trying times

Did you allocate time in your diary?

.................................................................................

What happened exactly at that time to stop you doing what you planned?

.................................................................................

Did you follow the suggested Dos and Don'ts?

.................................................................................

How can you ensure success next time?

.................................................................................

## Step Five

Repeat the activity every week for the rest of your life! If this seems a little ambitious, try one week per month for a while.

## Step Six

After some time, re-evaluate your progress.

- Do you think you could allot *more* time to your developmental activity?
- Is it taking up *too much* time?

Adjust your schedule accordingly but, whatever you do, don't give up your activity completely.

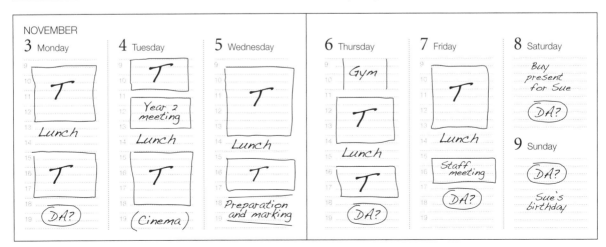

# Be my coach

## An interactive strategy to help you achieve your goals

### Rationale

Making use of an interpersonal approach to setting personal goals can help you achieve them more effectively. The motivation comes from commitment to interaction with another person, in the same way that going to a class, rather than teaching yourself, can help you learn a language.

### Activity

To set weekly goals for a month and work with a 'coach' to help motivate you to achieve them, even though you are working on your own.

### Step One

Find a coach. This person can be a friend or acquaintance, or your partner. They could be a colleague, too, although this activity can work better if the coach is not part of your work situation. The coach needs to be willing to meet/chat online/e-mail you once a week for a month for about 20 minutes each time.

### Step Two

Set yourself some goals you want to achieve for the week and write them down as in the example Pro-forma opposite. Assign a time for each one. There are check boxes to tick if the item is done and a space for comments, which you will fill in later.

- The goals can be classroom related (as in 1 and 2), related to general development (3) or practical career/job issues (4).
- You could add personal goals, too, if you want. For example: *Send my sister a birthday card.*
- The goals should be things you would like to achieve, but there is a chance you won't, as you may not perceive them as urgent. *Go to work on Thursday* wouldn't be a goal, in this sense!

### Step Three

E-mail your goals to your coach or hand them over on a piece of paper. The coach should simply acknowledge receipt. They shouldn't comment.

### Step Four

Arrange to meet or e-mail your coach at a specific time at the end of the week, to report on what you have achieved.

| My goals | | | |
|---|---|---|---|
| **What?** | **When?** | **Done** | **Comments** |
| **1** *Get some feedback from my morning intermediate class.* | Wednesday | | |
| **2** *Use a DVD in class with my advanced evening group, as they have requested this.* | Friday | | |
| **3** *Read three articles from Modern English Teacher.* | Tuesday morning | | |
| **4** *Fill in the job application form for summer school job.* | Monday evening | | |

### Step Five

At the end of the week, when you make contact with your coach, hand in or send the completed form, with notes on what you have or haven't achieved and comments. The coach can prompt you, if they feel you could explain more, but this isn't essential. The role of the coach is principally to make sure you report back, rather than offer advice or evaluate.

### Step Six

Do the same for the next three weeks. You will probably find yourself transferring some of the *not done* items from one week to the next, as well as adding new goals.

### Step Seven

At the end of the four weeks, thank your coach and offer to do the same for them if they are teachers.

### Step Eight

Reflect: Has this procedure helped you achieve more than you would have otherwise? Why? Why not?

# Why I am a teacher

## Thinking positively about being a teacher

### Rationale

Reminding yourself of the good things about being a teacher will help you feel more relaxed about dealing with small day-to-day challenges and irritations. A good activity to do when you are feeling negative about your job!

### Activity

To help bring to mind the many good reasons you are a teacher and compare teaching with another job.

### Step One

For each of the statements, put a tick in the 'Teacher' column of the Pro-forma below if it is true for you. Add three more reasons at the bottom if you can.

**Me and my job**

|  | Teacher | New job |
|---|---|---|
| I get a sense of satisfaction from helping people progress. |  |  |
| I like working with people. |  |  |
| I am paid well. |  |  |
| I like the variety in the job. |  |  |
| I'm good at teaching. |  |  |
| I have long holidays. |  |  |
| Teachers are respected in my country. |  |  |
| It's a very secure job. |  |  |
| I like the challenge. |  |  |
| I enjoy working with my colleagues. |  |  |
| I can be creative. |  |  |
| I am my own boss a lot of the time. |  |  |
| I have fun at work. |  |  |
| I am seldom bored. |  |  |
|  |  |  |
|  |  |  |
|  |  |  |

### Step Two

Count up your ticks. You probably found you had at least six. If you are still not convinced, try Step Three.

### Step Three

Imagine you weren't a teacher. What would you be? Return to the checklist and repeat the exercise for your new job. If your new job gets more ticks, think about changing jobs! On the other hand, liking what you do and doing what you like aren't so different, are they?

# My favourite teacher

## Role models from your school days

### Rationale

Reflecting on powerful role models from your past helps you to understand the teacher you have become.

### Activity

To think about your favourite teacher at school and how you compare to them.

### Step One

Read this description.

**My favourite teacher**

*He was my German teacher. He shared stories with us about his life and had a great sense of humour even when doctors had told him to give up smoking and he was obliged to suck lollipops all day! I always felt he took an interest in me personally. He was encouraging, too, and made me push myself. I'm not sure if everyone in the class felt that, though. I think he may have been less interested in the students who were not so keen on learning the language. He was demanding, too, giving us regular tests and encouraging a competitive atmosphere in the class, which I thought was fun. The materials he used were not original, I think, though he was happy to help us translate a German pop song when we brought one to class. I remember I felt good in his classes.*

### Step Two

Write a description of your favourite teacher from your school days.

### Step Three

Read through what you have written and consider these questions:

- Would your students say the same about you/your classes now?
- Does the teacher you have written about have the same style/approach/beliefs as you?
- Was your favourite teacher your classmates' favourite, too?

Your answers will help you become aware of how a powerful model from your past can shape your present.

### Step Four

Repeat Steps Two and Three, thinking about your *least favourite teacher*. How have they shaped the teacher you have become?

# The Magnificent Seven

## You and six teachers you know

### Rationale

Considering how teachers differ, and what kind of teacher you are, helps you to empathise with colleagues and see your own development more clearly.

### Activity

To think about different kinds of teacher and which types of teacher development activity would suit each one.

---

### Step One

Read the descriptions of the six teachers on this page.

### Step Two

Award between one and five stars according to how far you identify with each.

### Step Three

Recommend one development activity from the personal checklist on page 20 in the introduction to this circle, which you think would benefit each of these teachers.

### Step Four

Add a description of *you* in the seventh box, plus a rating and a recommendation for yourself.

### Step Five

Carry out your recommendation to yourself from Step Four.

---

**Six teachers and me**

**Jim** is a very busy person. He is always attending workshops and meeting other teachers. He is full of enthusiasm in the staffroom, keen to share ideas with other teachers and talk about teaching and students. The other day I found him surfing the net for sites for new materials.

Star rating:

Recommendation:

---

**Jeremy** is interested in doing lots of courses. He has invested a lot in training. The other day I saw him filling in an application for an MA TESOL course online. In the staffroom he likes talking about the courses he is doing or planning to do.

Star rating:

Recommendation:

---

**Jane** is always talking about her students and their progress. She likes using materials she has prepared specially for them. Yesterday I saw her making a cut-up reading activity about that earthquake using a text and pictures she had found on the internet. She said I was welcome to use it, too, if I wanted.

Star rating:

Recommendation:

---

**Nancy** is very keen on social events with students and teachers. Last week she organised a trip to see a play in English with the students. Her classes sound like fun. We can hear the students laughing and shouting from the other end of the school.

Star rating:

Recommendation:

---

**Scott** seems quiet. He doesn't say much in staff meetings and doesn't spend a lot of time in the teachers' room. He seems to be very popular with students. I think he goes away a lot at weekends. Someone told me he is really into mountain climbing.

Star rating:

Recommendation:

---

**Penny** complains a lot, especially about all the extra work we have to do 'unpaid' and how there is no chance of promotion for her. She's also quite sarcastic about the management of the school. Quite funny, though. She was telling me the other day how she was thinking of leaving teaching and finding a new job.

Star rating:

Recommendation:

---

**Me**

Star rating:

Recommendation

# What colour teacher are you?

## Looking at the way you think

### Rationale

This activity helps you reflect on your own *thinking style* and how it might influence your teaching and your development as a teacher.

### Activity

To decide what 'colour' your thinking style is and be aware of others.

### Step One

Read the information below about brain colours.

Psychologist Ned Hermann divides the brain into four sections, and proposes that people tend to think predominantly in one of the four sections: blue, yellow, green or red.

**Your brain colour**

| BLUE<br>Left brain – rational<br>You are logical and analytical. You like to get straight to the point. You listen attentively. You are realistic and independent. You may appear distant and arrogant. Your favourite question is: *Why?* | YELLOW<br>Right brain – rational<br>You are creative and intuitive. You see the big picture rather than the details. You generate ideas. You are independent and like variety. You tend to gesticulate. You can appear impatient and unrealistic. Your favourite question is: *What for?* |
|---|---|
| GREEN<br>Left brain – emotional<br>You are organized and well ordered. You like to plan and don't like interruptions. You are meticulous and can be upset by risk taking. You are very observant. You may appear inflexible and cautious. Your favourite questions are: *When, where, how many?* | RED<br>Right brain – emotional<br>You are sociable and intuitive. People and teams are important to you. You like to personalise. You may appear gossipy and manipulative. You feel strongly about injustice and dislike coldness in others. Your favourite question is: *Who?* |

### Step Two

According to the descriptions in the four boxes, decide to what extent each description fits you. Allocate up to five stars for each section: no stars if it is 'not you at all', five stars if the description describes you very well. Write your stars at the top of the Pro-forma opposite.

### Step Three

Look at your stars and see what the dominant colour of your brain is. You will probably find you are a mix of colours, with some more dominant than others.

### Step Four

Think about a colleague or colleagues you know well and do the same for them.

### Step Five

Consider the following questions:
- What kind of professional development activities will suit your colour?
- What are the strengths and weaknesses of teachers of your colour?
- How does your colour affect your teaching style?
- What are the strengths and weaknesses of your colleagues' colours?

Make notes in the Pro-forma, which has been started for you with some examples.

**Your teaching colour**

| BLUE<br>Star rating: | YELLOW<br>Star rating: |
|---|---|
| **Activities**<br>*Needs analysis, problem solving, planning and organising ...*<br><br>**Strengths and weaknesses**<br><br>**Teaching style** | **Activities**<br>*Experiments, trying out new methods, learning about new technology ...*<br><br>**Strengths and weaknesses**<br><br>**Teaching style** |
| **GREEN**<br>Star rating: | **RED**<br>Star rating: |
| **Activities**<br>*Syllabus design, writing tests, resources management ...*<br><br>**Strengths and weaknesses**<br><br>**Teaching style** | **Activities**<br>*Teacher observation, team teaching, feedback from students ...*<br><br>**Strengths and weaknesses**<br><br>**Teaching style** |

### Variation

Think about the brain colours of your students. Do Steps Four and Five, thinking about your students and how they *learn*.

# The Johari Window

**Four versions of you**

## Rationale

The Johari Window is a tool for helping you to think about yourself and your teaching.

## Activity

Reflecting on the teacher and person you are and the way others see you.

## Step One

Look at the first grid opposite and read about the Johari Window below.

> There are four ways of viewing yourself and your actions through the Johari Window:
>
> - **The open self** is the self everyone sees, you and other people.
> - **The blind self** is what others see but you yourself don't. It is often revealed in observation and feedback.
> - **The secret self** is the opposite, what you know about yourself and others don't. You can choose to reveal secrets, so they become part of the open self.
> - **The hidden self** is the part of you which no-one knows about, neither you nor others, until it surfaces. *'I didn't know you had it in you.' 'Neither did I!'* Unexpected challenges can help reveal the hidden self.

## Step Two

Think about your own teaching or other area of your life. Write an example in each of the four boxes in a grid like the one opposite. A second grid has been filled in with some examples, to help you get started.

## Step Three

Reflect on the *secret self*: What would happen if you revealed the secret you have written down in the secret self box? What would the advantages and disadvantages be?

## Step Four

Reflect on the *blind self*: Who helped you to 'see' and how? Did you benefit from seeing? If so, how? Would you like to know more about your blind self?

## Step Five

Reflect on the *hidden self*: How did you find it? What was the situation, what were the circumstances, who was involved?

### The Johari Window

|  | Known to self | Unknown to self |
|---|---|---|
| Known to others | Open | Blind |
| Unknown to others | Secret | Hidden |

### My Johari Window

|  | Known to self | Unknown to self |
|---|---|---|
| Known to others | Open<br><br>*I like to use music in my classes.* | Blind<br><br>*I used to stare at people and unnerve them. I didn't realise this until a colleague pointed it out to me.* |
| Unknown to others | Secret<br><br>*I find one of my students really hard to understand when he speaks. I've never had the courage to tell him.* | Hidden<br><br>*I invented bedtime stories for my children when they were young.* |

## Step Six

Your responses to the questions in Steps Three to Five will help you understand how you have changed and can change more as a teacher and, perhaps, as a person. Choose one of the three sections of the window you have thought about and commit to an action which will help you look again through the Johari Window. Write what you plan to do, and do it.

## Note

The name 'Johari' is derived from combining the two names of its inventors, Joseph Luft and Harry Ingram.

# Tea and two biscuits

## An activity for challenging stress

### Rationale

Thinking carefully and objectively about the causes of stress can help you generate more positive feelings. Writing things down systematically, and alone, gives you time and personal space to do this.

### Activity

To help you understand your stress, and work out a plan of action to deal with it.

### Step One

For this activity, follow the Steps and make notes in the Pro-forma opposite. Give yourself time and a quiet environment to do this. At home on the sofa rather than at your desk at work, for example, and with a cup of tea and maybe two biscuits. Don't worry about crumbs on the paper!

### Step Two

Think of something that is causing you stress at the moment in your work. State the problem clearly and specifically.

### Step Three

Add some information and examples to illustrate the problem you have identified. Use these three prompts to help you: When do you feel this stress? Where? Who is involved?

### Step Four

Generate possible solutions. At this stage, just brainstorm. Don't rule any ideas out. Make notes under these three headings:

- Avoiding/leaving the situation
- Altering the situation
- Altering your perception of the situation

### Step Five

Evaluate the different options and choose one or two.

### Step Six

Develop a plan of action. What will you do? When and where? Who will it involve?

---

**Solutions for stress**

**The problem**

**The details**

When:

Where:

Who:

**The solutions**

Avoid:

Alter the situation:

Alter the perception of the situation:

**The action plan**

What:

When and where:

Who:

# Mirror, mirror

## What do you think of your teaching?

### Rationale

This self-observation task is designed to help you evaluate your own teaching by focusing on three key areas: your planning, your performance in class, and your learners' performance in class.

### Activity

To reflect on a range of aspects of your teaching and identify specific areas for future self-observation.

### Step One

Decide on a class you would like to observe yourself teaching. It can be any you teach, though it can be more interesting to choose one you feel is problematic in some way.

### Step Two

Copy the Pro-forma opposite. It will help you to focus your observation and give you a written record of it.

### Step Three

Make notes in Section 1 of the Pro-forma *before* the class.

### Step Four

Immediately *after* the class, complete Sections 2–4. Award yourself a mark out of ten in each section. This will help you to 'get off the fence' and really pinpoint strengths and shortcomings.

### Step Five

Finally complete Section 5 of the Pro-forma.

### Step Six

Decide on a specific area to focus on in a future self-observation. Use your notes in Section 5 to help you. For example, if you have decided you want to improve the way you correct students, you can make this the single theme of a future self-observation.

---

**Self-observation: diagnosis and reflection**

**Section 1 – Class information**

Level:                      Date:

Class profile:

Aims:

| Section 2 – Planning | My score |
|---|---|
| Did I anticipate the problems my students had? | |
| Were the aims appropriate for these students? | |
| Did I achieve my aims (linguistic and communicative)? | |

| Section 3 – Teacher performance | My score |
|---|---|
| Did the students understand my instructions? | |
| Were all my students catered for? | |
| Did I vary interaction patterns between students? | |
| How much did I talk? Was any of my talk 'inappropriate'? | |
| How/when were students corrected? Was there any peer or self-correction? | |

| Section 4 – Student performance | My score |
|---|---|
| Was there a positive learning environment or not (teacher rapport, humour, listening to students with interest, inappropriate use of L1 by students, bad atmosphere)? | |
| How authentic was the communication? | |
| How much did my students talk (to other students/to me)? | |

| Section 5 – Conclusions | My score |
|---|---|
| In what areas do I need to improve? | |

# Go with the flow

## Looking at student motivation in your class

### Rationale

Motivation is arguably the most important factor affecting how much your students learn. Challenge is a crucial element of motivation, so it is a good idea to look at your teaching on a regular basis in terms of how easy or difficult the work is for your students.

### Activity

To reflect on how your students are reacting to a lesson and raise your awareness of the level of challenge in your class.

### Note

Csikszentmihalyi has defined 'flow' or 'satisfaction' as an optimum state of affairs where challenge and skill are matched.

- Low challenge combined with high skill and a lot of confidence leads to frustration and boredom ('flight').
- High challenge with low skill and a lack of confidence leads to anxiety ('fight').

This can be represented in the first diagram opposite.

---

### Step One

On a piece of A4 paper, sketch a diagram like the one opposite.

### Step Two

As you are teaching, map the different lesson stages and activities into the chart, according to your perceptions. There is a completed example opposite.

### Step Three

After the lesson, look at your chart. Ask yourself the following questions:

- How could I achieve more *flow*, less *flight* and less *fight* next time?
- How could I move some of the items in 'Flight' and 'Fight' into the middle 'Flow' section, matching both challenge and skill for my students?

### Variations

Instead of thinking of the group as a whole, focus on one individual and map their 'flow' in your lesson.

Fill in a 'flow diagram' for your own life as a teacher. When do you feel you are in each of the three zones

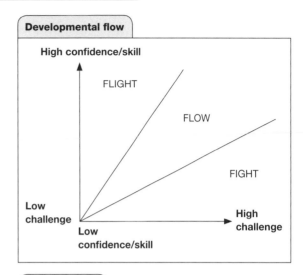

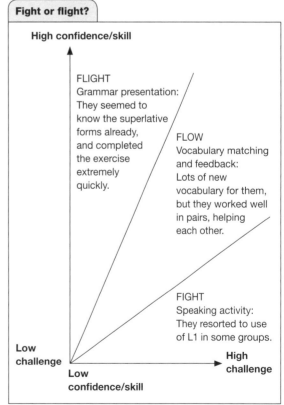

# The icing on the cake

## Improving your English

### Rationale

The better your English, the more confident you will feel, both in the classroom and communicating with other speakers of English outside the classroom. This activity helps you to focus your efforts where you feel they are most needed.

### Activity

To evaluate different aspects of your English and decide what you would like to improve on.

### Step One

Read and respond to the statements in the 'My English' questionnaire opposite.

This is a *performance/importance* questionnaire. For each statement you give two ratings: the *performance* rating, according to how well you perform in that aspect of your English, and the *importance* rating, according to how important it is for you to perform well in that aspect. For example: for the last statement, '*I can read a novel in English*', you might feel that you can do this quite comfortably and score 3 or 4 on *performance*, but that it is not important for you (you don't like reading novels and never need to), so you score 0 or 1 on *importance*.

### Step Two

In the spaces provided, add other aspects of your English you would like to rate, which are not listed. These could be more specific examples of the aspects already listed. For example:

> *Drilling students for pronunciation in class*
> *Writing informal e-mails to colleagues in English*

Rate the new items for performance and importance.

### Step Three

Decide on **one** aspect you would like to improve and how you will do it. Use the *performance/importance* scores to help you do this, by looking at where you have a lower score for *performance* than *importance*. Write down what you decide to do.

**Improving my performance**

I have decided to improve my ....................................

- *How?* ...................................................
- *When?* ..................................................
- *Who with?* ...............................................
- *How will I measure my progress?*

   ....................................................

**My English**

| | Performance (0 = not at all true, 5 = completely true) | Importance (0 = not at all important, 5 = very important) |
|---|---|---|
| I feel comfortable speaking in English when I am teaching. | | |
| I can understand the coursebook I use. | | |
| I feel comfortable speaking to other non-native speakers. | | |
| I feel comfortable speaking to native speakers. | | |
| I can communicate effectively in writing. | | |
| My pronunciation is good enough to be always understood. | | |
| I can understand films and TV in English. | | |
| I can read a novel in English. | | |
| | | |
| | | |
| | | |

# *Voda ne perliva prozim*

## A lesson in another language

### Rationale

Putting yourself in your learners' shoes by reminding yourself how you react and feel in a language lesson is a very powerful way of provoking reflection and reassessment of your own teaching.

### Activity

To experience a language lesson and consider the implications for your own teaching.

---

### Step One

You are going to participate in a lesson in another language. It can be one you already speak partly, or a completely new language. Decide the language and find a teacher (your choice may be defined by what is available to you). It can be a group class (you may have to sign up for more than one hour) or an individual class.

### Step Two

Establish the time and place for the class.

### Step Three

At some point before the class, take five minutes to complete the sentence stems opposite about your feelings and expectations in the 'Before' column.

### Step Four

Attend the class. Participate as 'naturally' as possible, but make a few notes about your reactions to jog your memory, if you feel it helpful.

### Step Five

Shortly after the class, make notes in the 'After' column of the grid about what actually happened in relation to your expectations. Add any other thoughts and insights that occur to you.

### Step Six

Read your notes and perhaps discuss them with a colleague. What change(s) will you make to your own teaching as a result of this experience? List them in the Pro-forma, too.

### Note

*Voda ne perliva prozim* means 'Still water, please!' in Czech.

| Feelings and expectations | Before | After |
|---|---|---|
| I hope to learn… | | |
| I hope we don't… | | |
| I hope we do… | | |
| Thinking about the class, I feel… | | |
| I hope the teacher… | | |
| (for a group class) I hope the other students… | | |

| Thoughts and insights |
|---|
| |

| Changes |
|---|
| |

# You and your students

## The second circle

Who better to help you develop as a teacher than your own students? These are the people who work with you most and know you best as a teacher. Engaging in developmental activities which involve your learners will benefit both you and them.

We are now in the second circle, where the activities can again be carried out without help from other teachers. The same advantages therefore apply as in circle one, although the level of challenge increases slightly, as you now need to engage with others. Your students are a captive audience, of course, so you have plenty of influence over what happens in class. However, when you are finding out their needs, asking for feedback and experimenting with new ideas, you will have to think carefully about how best to communicate with them, so that they feel a sense of partnership.

This is the circle where *your* development and *their* development go explicitly hand in hand. The activities here:

- can be used in any teaching context;
- are simple to carry out;
- require very little or no extra preparation.

Developmental activities with your students work on the S and E motivations in the RISE model (see the introduction to the first circle and the activity on page 22): Self-improvement and Enjoyment. However, you may find you can also share your experiences with colleagues in the staffroom, in writing or workshops, for example, and gain Recognition.

Opposite is a checklist of things you can do and which involve your students. Which have you already done? Which have you not thought of doing? Which might you like to concentrate on? Which of the things are of particular interest to you? Read through the list and give yourself a score for each item.

This second circle is comprised of three sections and we begin by first looking at what our students need.

### Your students' needs

What we know about our students can be divided into a number of categories, all of which can influence how we teach them.

- Personality
- Personal life
- Likes and dislikes
- Hobbies and interests
- Learning styles and intelligences
- Strengths and weaknesses in English

---

**Personal checklist**

There are things you can do with your students in mind, to develop yourself and your teaching. Read down the list.

- Give yourself a score from 0-5 for each item, according to how often you do it (0 = 'never done this', 5 = 'done this a lot').
- Then complete the right-hand column, adding a tick (✔) where appropriate, if you would like to try something, or do more of it

| Things I have done (or not done) … | Score (0-5) | (✔) |
|---|---|---|
| Made some new material | | |
| Used authentic materials (DVD, internet, newspapers, etc) | | |
| Got feedback from my students | | |
| Talked to my students socially | | |
| Experimented with a new method, approach or technique | | |
| Got to know more about an individual learner | | |
| Held tutorials with my students | | |
| Learnt my students' mother tongue | | |
| Done a needs analysis with my students | | |
| Got my students to teach me something | | |
| Learnt about my students' culture | | |
| Recorded my students on tape or video | | |

**Comment**
Looking at this list should help identify areas of particular interest for you (or that you hadn't perhaps thought of) and will help you decide which activities you would most like to do.

---

- Cultural background
- Attitude to learning English/to being at school
- Reasons for learning English

The extent to which we are able to, or wish to, cater for individuality in the class will depend on the size of class and the culture we come from or are working in. In some cultures, considerable emphasis is placed on attempting to tailor learning to individual needs. In others, there is more emphasis on achieving collective goals.

The first two activities help you find out more about your learners as individuals. In *Dear teacher…* you ask the students to reflect on themselves, while in *Man overboard!* you do the opposite, and you reflect on one of your students. Finding out about the priorities of individuals is an important first step forward for teachers. An important second step in class teaching, as opposed to one-to-one teaching, is for students to become aware of how their individual needs will fit in with the rest of the group. Negotiating what we might call 'group needs' is addressed in the activities *How can we help each other?* and *Needs from the heart.*

When you are teaching children and business English students, the classes are usually paid for by parents or the students' companies. The students are the 'users' of the service and the parents or the company are the 'clients'. In these situations, it can be important to find out about the expectations and needs of the clients as well as the users. You may find you can adapt these activities in your own classes to incorporate them.

### Getting feedback

When was the last time you got some feedback from your students? It may seem like common sense to find out what students think of your classes, so why isn't it common practice? One reason for this is that teachers are naturally anxious about asking students for feedback. Criticism, however well-meant, can be hard to accept in all areas of our life! In many schools, your learners will be asked formally to give some feedback on the classes, often through a questionnaire distributed at the end of term. This procedure can be useful for the teacher, the students and the school, but there are two shortcomings. The first is timing. The feedback comes too late to be acted upon. The second is that this manner of collecting feedback can create a sense that the students are passive recipients of the teaching rather than active participants.

Getting regular feedback throughout the course will help you become aware of possible problems in advance, inspire confidence in your learners and increase your confidence as a teacher.

The activities in this section have three key features:

- They promote a collaborative attitude, where the classroom is seen as place where teacher and students can work together to make improvements. With this in mind, you will find it easier to get feedback, accept it and act on it.
- They are designed to be easy to use, because asking for feedback is difficult.
- They incorporate a variety of approaches, because *when* you get feedback and *how* you get feedback will have an effect on the kind of response you get.

The most important thing about feedback is to get some! You spend a lot of time feeding your learners, you deserve the chance to get 'fed back' in return!

### Trying something new

John Fanselow suggests that teachers should incorporate changes and surprises into their teaching, to keep students engaged and alert. It is also a good strategy for teacher

development. We can group possible changes in teacher behaviour into five categories:

- Change who – teacher becomes student, student becomes teacher.
- Change where – change the room layout and your position, teach somewhere else.
- Change how – vary the techniques you use and your modes of working.
- Change when – vary the sequence of your lesson plan.
- Change what – teach something completely different, varying your materials.

Trying something new can involve *observing* what you do, *changing* what you do, *reflecting* on what you do, *keeping a record* of what you do, or a combination of any of these. For example, if you are wondering about the best way to combine your students in pairwork activities, you can do the following:

- Observe your students in pairwork one day and make notes on how they perform.
- Try out different types of pairing, eg strong with weak students, strong with strong, extrovert with introvert, and so on.
- Devise a questionnaire for the students, asking about their preferred partners for pairwork.
- Ask other teachers what they do.
- Reflect on the above.

Training courses for teachers often prompt you to try out these kinds of changes. The activities here help you to explore some of these possibilities. They involve experimenting with class management, teacher roles, methods and materials. In some cases, you will find you want to adopt the change. In other cases, you find you don't, but you will understand your current practice better as a result of trying something different. Either way, experimenting with change can be a powerful developmental tool for you and an enjoyable adventure for your students.

Innovations work best if they relate to something that specifically concerns you in your teaching. These activities are examples for you to try out, so you should feel completely free to adapt the ideas and use them simply as a springboard in your own personal situation.

The activities in this circle help you to develop through gaining a much clearer understanding of your students and the effect you have on them. You will find that you both have quite a lot of fun, too, particularly with the activities in the *Trying something new* section.

You will no doubt also be keen to talk to colleagues about your experiences, which provides us with a natural link to the activities in circle three, *You and your colleagues.*

# Dear teacher ...

## Casual needs analysis

**Rationale**

A less formal approach to needs analysis can often elicit more information than traditional form-filling and questionnaires.

**Activity**

You find out the background and needs of the individual learners in your class.

**Step One**

Write a letter to your students, adapting the model below to your own teaching situation.

**Step Two**

In class, get the students to read the letter. Make sure they have understood it by eliciting examples of what they could write in reply.

**Step Three**

Ask them to write you a reply. Tell them they can write in English, or a mixture of English and their own language.

**Step Four**

Collect the replies. Read them and reply to each one individually. If you want to let the students read each other's letters and your replies, pin them up around the class and invite the students to walk round and read them.

**Variation**

You could do the activity via e-mail.

### A letter to your students

Dear Students,

I am your teacher. I want to help you improve your English. I have been teaching English for four years. I like playing tennis and listening to music. My favourite singer is Tracy Chapman. I like my job, although it is sometimes quite difficult. I am always interested in ways of improving.

I want to make these classes useful and interesting for you. Can you help me by telling me something about yourself, your life and your experience of learning English? Can you tell me why learning English is important for you and some things you would like to do in class? Thank you.

Yours,

Liria

# Man overboard!

## Rescuing the 'missing' student

**Rationale**

The 'man overboard' (or woman, boy or girl!) is the student in your class who does not participate, is often absent or late, and seems generally unmotivated. You would like to help them or at least find out more about them.

**Activity**

You think about a student who is not getting much out of your class.

**Step One**

Before class, write down everything you know about the student in the first column of the Pro-forma below.

**Step Two**

Think about what else you would like to know, and write questions in the second column. Read your questions and choose three which are the most interesting/easy to find the answer to.

**Step Three**

Give yourself one week to find the answers to your three questions, and write the answers in the third column. You may need to talk to other teachers, to other students, or the student in question, to find the information you need.

**Step Four**

Now look at the information you have in the grid. Think of a strategy or activity which might help engage your student. Write it down and try it next week.

### Student rescue

|  | I know | I'd like to know | What I found out |
|---|---|---|---|
| Personal data |  |  |  |
| Interests |  |  |  |
| Behaviour in my class |  |  |  |
| Contacts/incidents with the student (in or outside class) |  |  |  |
| Behaviour in other classes |  |  |  |
| Other information |  |  |  |

# How can we help each other?

**Group needs analysis**

## Rationale

It is useful for you and your students to be aware of how learning is affected by the social dynamic of the classroom. Results come from the interaction of three players: the student, their classmates and you, the teacher.

## Activity

Your students complete and discuss a questionnaire about how to make the most of themselves, their classmates and their teacher as resources for learning English in class.

---

## Step One

Hand out the questionnaire opposite. Ask the students to read Sections 1 and 2 and add at least one statement to each section.

## Step Two

Ask the students to rank each statement in these sections as follows: 5 = very important, 0 = not at all important.

## Step Three

Ask them to compare and discuss their rankings and their additions.

## Step Four

Get some feedback on this. Listen, mostly. Highlight consensus, and lack of it, where appropriate.

## Step Five

Now ask the students to rank each statement in Section 3, *How can the teacher help me?*, in the same way as with Sections 1 and 2, adding their own suggestions.

## Step Six

Hold a 'pyramid' discussion. The students work in pairs and agree on a 'top six' for this section. Then pairs combine into groups of four and negotiate further, if necessary, to agree on a new top six. Finally the whole class negotiate, including you, and you all vote on a final top six.

## Step Seven

The students make a poster with the six top tips for the teacher. Put up the poster in class if you can.

| Making the most of my English class | Score (0-5) 5 = very important, 0 = not at all important |
|---|---|
| **1 How can I help myself in class?** | |
| Use English as much as possible. | |
| Ask questions. | |
| Go to class as often as possible and arrive on time. | |
| Participate as much as possible. | |
| *Add more suggestions:* | |
| **2 How can my classmates help me improve my English?** | |
| Listen and talk to me. | |
| Help me when I have difficulties. | |
| Correct me when I speak English. | |
| Do exercises with me in class. | |
| *Add more suggestions:* | |
| **3 How can the teacher help me improve my English?** | |
| Listen and talk to me. | |
| Give me opportunities to talk and listen in English. | |
| Give me encouragement. | |
| Make the lessons enjoyable. | |
| Make the lessons useful. | |
| Make the lessons challenging. | |
| Give me opportunities to read and write in English. | |
| Show me how to do things in English. | |
| Help me when I have difficulties. | |
| Help me learn new vocabulary and grammar. | |
| Correct me when I speak English. | |
| Help me pronounce English better. | |
| *Add more suggestions:* | |

# Needs from the heart

## Students help plan your lessons

### Rationale

If students are involved in setting objectives and choosing tasks themselves, classes will be more relevant and motivating. Their willingness to engage in this kind of activity may vary according to age, culture and their reasons for learning English.

### Activity

Your students participate in planning a lesson or series of lessons.

### Step One

Elicit from your students some things they would like to do, or need to do, in English. They might say, for example, 'understand films', 'talk about my home town', 'read news stories on the internet' or 'product presentation'. Elicit quite a few and write them on the board.

### Step Two

Draw a heart shape in the centre of the board or OHP transparency. Ask the students to choose one of the items from Step One which they would like to work on, taking a vote if necessary. Write the item they decide inside the heart.

### Step Three

In pairs, the students discuss possible activities in class which would help them improve in the chosen aim. For example, if they chose 'talk about my home town' they might suggest 'listen to someone talking about their home town', 'learn words and phrases to describe a town', or 'practise talking with a partner about our home town'.

### Step Four

Get feedback. Add the suggestions to the board in the form of a mind map or spidergram. You can, of course, prompt and make suggestions of your own. See the example below, which is taken from a business class.

### Step Five

Get the students to copy the finished spidergram (or photocopy it, if you have used an OHT). You can also get two students to make a poster-sized version, to put up in class for reference.

### Step Six

Agree with the students an approximate timeframe to complete what has been proposed. It may be one lesson or a whole series of lessons.

### Step Seven

You have created a mini-syllabus. Now make sure you do it! Use your poster/OHT/students' copies to tick things off as you do them.

**Planning a presentation**

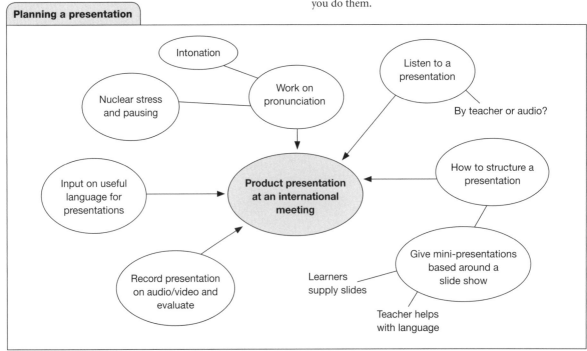

# Three against one

## Balancing positive and negative feedback

### Rationale
Students can find it difficult to criticise their teacher. And for the person receiving feedback (the teacher, in this case), 'suggestions' are easier to act on than criticisms. This activity works well mid-course.

### Activity
The students express what they like about the class and suggest improvements.

### Step One
At the beginning of a lesson (midway through a term or course), distribute the questionnaire below and ask the students to complete the first part. Complete one yourself, too.

| Three-against-one questionnaire | |
|---|---|
| **1 Three things I like about the class:** | |
| ☺ | |
| ☺ | |
| ☺ | |
| One suggestion I have for the teacher: | |
| | |
| **2 One more 'like':** | |
| One more suggestion: | |

### Step Two
Ask the students to stand up with their questionnaire and walk around the room. When you call out *Stop!* they should stop and talk to the person nearest them about what they have written. After a minute or two, call out *Move!* and then *Stop!* again. The students now talk to a different person. Repeat until the students have talked to three or four classmates (about five minutes in total). Join in the activity yourself if you would like to.

### Step Three
Tell the students to sit down and think about their classmates' likes and suggestions. They choose their favourite 'like' and their favourite suggestion from a classmate and add them to their questionnaire in the space provided.

### Step Four
Collect the questionnaires. Thank the students and tell them you will read them after class.

### Step Five
At the next class, give the students feedback on their questions or suggestions. Highlight at least one suggestion you will definitely be implementing.

# Face down, face up

## Comments on cards prompt student feedback

### Rationale
Getting students to discuss their reactions to the class helps them to elaborate on thoughts more than in writing, and to become aware of other students' opinions. Prompts will help to get them thinking and talking.

### Activity
The students discuss their opinions about the class by responding to prompts on cards while you listen to their comments.

### Step One
Before class, cut out the prompt cards below, adding two of your own. Make one set of cards per three or four students.

### Step Two
Put the students into groups of three or four, with one set of cards for each, face down. Explain that the cards contain comments students sometimes make about English classes. One student should turn over the first card and read it to the group, who then discuss the statement, saying if they agree or disagree. Encourage them to refer to examples from lessons to support their points. When they are ready, they turn over another statement and discuss it. Begin by starting a discussion of one of the statements as a whole-class activity.

### Step Three
After about ten minutes, tell the students to stop. Ask them to choose one of the statements (the one they found most interesting or the one which caused most disagreement, for example) and nominate a person to report back.

### Step Four
The spokesperson reports back to the class. You listen, and help with language if necessary, but *don't dispute* any of the points raised.

### Step Five
Thank the students, summarise any key points that emerged and promise to take their suggestions into account in future lessons.

| | |
|---|---|
| We should speak more in class. | We speak our own language too much in class. |
| I think the listening activities are too difficult. | Sometimes the lessons are too easy. |
| We learn useful vocabulary. | I wish the teacher would correct my mistakes more. |
| We could improve the appearance of the classroom. | The materials we use in class are interesting. |
| | |

# Pain and gain

## Comparing learning and fun

### Rationale

Can learning be fun? Are your students' ideas of fun the same as yours? You might be surprised by the feedback you get in this activity.

### Activity

Your students reflect on the different stages of a class they have had and rate them in terms of learning and enjoyment.

### Note

You need 15 minutes for this at the end of the lesson, so plan a shorter lesson.

### Step One

Elicit from the students the stages/activities in the lesson, and get them to write them in a Pro-forma (see the example opposite). You don't need to cover the whole lesson. Three or four stages are enough. Use the board or OHP to help you.

### Step Two

Ask the students to award each stage a score from 0-3, according to how useful and how enjoyable they thought it was. (0 = 'not useful', 3 = 'very useful'). Ask them to write some comments in the last column, such as:

- *I wanted more time on this.*
- *The examples were very helpful.*
- *This was fun because we spoke a lot.*

Do the same yourself.

### Step Three

In groups of three or four, the students discuss what they have written, while you monitor.

### Step Four

Collect the questionnaires and read them. Compare their responses to yours. Are there any differences? Write down the most important thing you have learned from this feedback. Share this with your students at the next class.

**Pain or gain**

| Lesson activity/stage (What we did) | Useful (0-3) | Enjoyable (0-3) | Comment |
|---|---|---|---|
| The class talking about holidays with the teacher. | | | |
| Listening to a CD with someone talking about their holidays and answering T/F questions. | | | |
| The teacher explaining how to form questions in English. | | | |
| Doing a gap-fill activity on question forms. | | | |
| Talking in pairs about our last holiday. | | | |
| The teacher discussing our mistakes after the speaking activity. | | | |
| | | | |
| | | | |

# Four fast feedback formats

## Quick, easy and effective

## Hot feedback
### How are you feeling?

This activity explores the affective side of learning. It gives you a quick snapshot of how students are feeling at a given point in the lesson. This is useful in itself and requires no specific follow-up.

### Step One

Stop the class at some point in the lesson. It can be at any moment: while you are addressing them or while they are working in pairs or groups.

### Step Two

Write on the board the following question:

*How are you feeling at the moment?*

Give out slips of paper and ask the students to write a few lines in response to the question. Tell them you want them to be honest and that the slips are anonymous. Give them a few minutes to do this.

### Step Three

Collect the slips of paper and read them after class, but don't feel you need to discuss them with the students.

## Cool feedback
### What can you remember?

This activity helps you understand what is memorable for students, not necessarily in terms of what they learnt but what they think about the lesson in hindsight.

### Step One

At the start of the lesson, write on the board the following question:

*What can you remember about the last class we had?*

### Step Two

Give out slips of paper and ask the students to write a few lines in response to the question. Tell them they can write any memories that come into their head:

- what they did, saw, said, learnt;
- the room, the people, the teacher;
- what they heard, something funny, anything.

Give them a prompt or two to help them focus.

### Step Three

Give them a few minutes to do this and do it yourself, too.

### Step Four

Tell the students to pin their pieces of paper on the wall for others to read, or pass them round. Join the students in reading and commenting on what they have written. Keep this light-hearted: don't write anything down, but make a mental note of everything.

## Feedback on learning
### What did you learn today?

*Input* rarely corresponds to *intake* in teaching. This activity helps you to see the lesson content through the students' eyes. You may (or may not) be surprised to find that your perceptions and those of your learners do not always coincide.

### Note

Allow ten minutes at the end of class for this.

### Step One

Ask the students to write down on a piece of paper *three* things they have learned or practised today. Do the same yourself.

### Step Two

Get the students to pass the papers round the class in a clockwise direction, reading each one as they go, until they get their own paper back, so they read everyone else's. If you have a large class, you can do this in smaller groups.

### Step Three

In pairs or small groups, the students discuss what they wrote and read. You read and listen, as you monitor the groups.

### Step Four

Write on the board *your* three things, and round off with a light-hearted plenary discussion highlighting any differences between you and the students and between different students.

## Feedback on fun
### What did you like best today?

This simple procedure helps you to understand where in the lesson the students are having fun, and if different students have different ideas of fun.

### Step One

Near the end of the class, write these two questions on the board:

- *What was the most fun part of the class today?*
- *Why?*

### Step Two

The students discuss the two questions in pairs or groups.

### Step Three

Hold a feedback discussion with the whole class.

### Variation

Substitute the word *fun* for *boring*.

# Learning from young learners

### They can give you feedback, too

## Rationale

Most young learners can give valuable and helpful feedback to teachers. What is more, they enjoy doing so. The questionnaire here can be translated in part or fully into the learners' first language if necessary.

## Activity

Your young learners give you mid-term or mid-course feedback on different aspects of the class.

## Step One

Distribute the questionnaire opposite to the children. If it is in English, make sure they understand it. Check the vocabulary and do some examples. Tell the children to complete the questionnaire individually. Tell them you would like them to be honest in their answers and that it will help you a lot: you will read them afterwards.

## Step Two

Collect the questionnaires and read them after class. Don't write on them but keep them safe. Act on what you find out.

## Step Three

Give the children their questionnaires back at the same stage the following term, for example. Tell them to read the questionnaires and change any answers they want to. Collect them again and read them.

## Stage Four

You may choose to follow Steps Two or Three with a discussion, if you feel this would be useful.

# Four fast feedback formats

- Write the day's activities on the board. The children stand next to the activity they enjoyed most. Make a mental note of their preferences, perhaps comment on them, and tell them to sit down.
- Make a chart which lists all the days you have a lesson and put it on the wall. At the end of each lesson, the children put different coloured stickers by the date of that lesson: a green sticker for 'a great day', blue for 'okay', red for 'not very good'.
- Write on the board in three columns: *I learned a lot today. I learned some things today. I didn't learn a lot today.* Leave the room, having asked the children to put a tick under the comment they think is true for them.
- Ask the children to rate the lessons privately in their notebooks, using the same marking scheme you use with them: ABC, or a mark out of 10, for example. When you collect *their* books to mark some of *their* work, look at *your* marks.

---

**My English class**

Name ................................................................................

**Read and draw stars.**

I like it a lot: ★★★   It's OK: ★★   I don't like it much: ★

| Doing exercises from the book | | Learning new words | |
|---|---|---|---|
| Writing stories | | Tests | |
| Games | | Speaking in English with my friends | |
| Reading stories with the teacher | | Watching videos | |

Tick ✔:

**When the teacher speaks ...**

I always understand.  ☐

I sometimes understand.  ☐

I never understand.  ☐

**When I don't understand, it's OK to ask the teacher.**

YES ☐    NO ☐    MAYBE ☐

**Choose a face:** ☺ ☺ ☹

| We work in groups. | We work alone. |
|---|---|
| We work in pairs. | We speak to everyone in the class. |

**Easy or difficult? Put the number in the 'Easy' box or the 'Difficult' box.**

1 Spelling
2 Listening to the teacher
3 Remembering words
4 Speaking

5 Understanding the CD
6 Reading on my own
7 Listening and repeating
8 Writing a story

| Easy ☺ | Difficult ☹ |
|---|---|
| | |

I want to do more ...................................................

## Acknowledgement

The young learner feedback activities are based on ideas from Nicola Meldrum.

# Together or alone?

## An experiment with groupwork writing

### Rationale
Experimenting with different ways of teaching helps you to understand what works best for you and your students. Students enjoy participating in 'experiments', which provide variety and give them the opportunity to reflect on and discuss how they learn best. Incorporating activities like this into your teaching shows them that you take their learning seriously.

### Activity
Your students compare working alone with working in a group on a writing task.

### Step One
Before class, choose an e-mail/letter-writing task from your coursebook or other source with two parts. For example, the task could be writing to complain about something and then writing a reply to the complaint, or writing an e-mail to a friend and then writing a reply.

### Step Two
Divide the class in half, and set the first part of the task.

> **Group A:** Ask them to complete the first part of the writing task individually.
>
> **Group B:** They complete the first part of the task in groups of three, with one person acting as scribe.

### Step Three
Collect the scripts from the Group A students and distribute them to each Group B student. Do the same for Group B, distributing their scripts to Group A, who should now be put in threes.

### Step Four
Tell the students to write the replies to the letters/e-mails they have been given. Group A are now working in threes and Group B individually.

### Step Five
After the writing tasks are completed, get the students to discuss in their groups (or new groups) the differences between the two ways of working, and which they preferred.

### Step Six
Round off with a plenary feedback session. What do the students have to say? Will the experiment cause you to change the way you teach writing?

# To pre-teach ... or not?

## An experiment with vocabulary in reading

### Rationale
The issue explored here – whether to pre-teach vocabulary or have the students work out meaning from context – is one which is very often debated by teachers and which provides an ideal activity for both research and innovation.

### Activity
You test and evaluate two different ways of reading and learning vocabulary in class.

### Step One
Before class, choose a text from your coursebook or other source. Decide on a set of ten words or phrases you want your students to learn from it.

### Step Two
Divide the class into two halves and tell them that both groups are going to read a text and learn some vocabulary, but in different ways. Tell them they have 20 minutes, at the end of which time they will have a short test on the text and the vocabulary.

> **Group A:** Give them the vocabulary list and some dictionaries. After ten minutes, give them the text to read, with the words underlined. The students work in pairs.
>
> **Group B:** Give them the text with the words underlined but no dictionaries. After ten minutes, give them the dictionaries. The students work in pairs.

### Step Three
Give all the students a copy of the text with comprehension questions (as in the coursebook, or your own if you prefer) and the ten underlined words taken out. (You will need to have prepared this.) Tell them to fill the blanks with the correct word, and answer the questions. Give them five minutes to complete the test on their own.

### Step Four
Put the answers to the test on the board or OHP, for the students to check. Which group got the best results on the test?

### Step Five
Put the students in groups of four, with two As and two Bs in each group. They discuss the differences between the two approaches, and which they preferred.

### Step Six
Round off with whole-class feedback. What do the students have to say? Will the experiment cause you to change the way you teach vocabulary with reading texts?

# Correction traffic lights
## Different ways of correcting speaking errors

### Rationale
If you are curious about experimenting with different ways of correcting your students, you will find this activity useful, as it helps you to learn about your students' preferences.

### Activity
You compare different approaches to correcting errors in speaking activities.

### Step One
Choose a speaking activity that will keep the students talking for 5–10 minutes, depending on their level. The activity could be a roleplay, a group discussion, or pair conversation. It is important that the activity allows the students to speak freely.

### Step Two
Divide the class into three groups: Red, Yellow and Green. Each group member should be identified with a colour sticker on their arm, or anywhere clearly visible. Tell the students that when they are speaking, you will be walking around listening but treating each colour differently.

| Red: | You will be correcting every mistake you hear them make. They can ask you for help. |
|---|---|
| Yellow: | You will not correct them at all. They can ask you for help. |
| Green: | You will not correct them at all. They can't ask you for help. |

### Step Three
Do the activity, correcting the students (or not) according to the criteria.

### Step Four
Put the students in groups of three (with each group containing one person of each colour). Get them to discuss the differences between the three ways of working and which they preferred.

### Step Five
Round off with whole-class feedback. You may find you want to change your approach to correcting errors after this, or you may find it reinforces your belief in your current approach.

# Interactive interrupting
## Offering new opportunities in listening practice

### Rationale
Many students find listening the most difficult skill, and report high levels of anxiety when doing listening activities in class, perhaps because common practice in coursebooks is to adopt a 'test-like' approach. Students typically listen to a recording and answer some questions afterwards. Here, they don't have to wait.

### Activity
Your students listen to a recording and interrupt, asking questions to clarify their understanding.

### Step One
Choose a listening text from your coursebook or other source, and prepare copies of the script if necessary and if you plan to give it out.

### Step Two
Do your usual **pre-listening** activities, to raise awareness of the topic/context and pre-teach the key language.

### Step Three
Do not set any **listening** task or questions. Instead, follow this procedure:
- Tell the students that you will start playing the recording and they should ask you to stop whenever they want to ask a question or comment on what they have heard.
- When a student asks you to stop the recording, you and the other students should listen to the question or comment, and respond as appropriate. Encourage other students to respond if they can, rather than *you*. Replay if necessary.
- Continue, until you have listened to the end of the recording.
- Play the recording again, this time without stopping, for students to listen to the whole text.

### Step Four
Give the students the script if you wish and carry out any **post-listening** follow-up work that you would normally do.

### Step Five
Put the students in groups of three. Get them to discuss what they thought were the pros and cons of listening in this way. Would they like to listen in this way in the future?

### Step Six
Round off with whole-class feedback. You may find you want to change your approach to listening after this, or it may reinforce your belief in your current approach.

# A VAK experiment

## Visual, Auditory and Kinaesthetic learning

### Rationale
This task helps your students to become aware of different learning styles and to consider which they prefer.

### Activity
The students work on a text in three different ways: visual, auditory and kinaesthetic.

### Step One
Choose a story-type text from your coursebook or other source: not too long, between 100 and 300 words. Photocopy it by itself on a bare white page with nothing around it.

### Step Two
Divide the class into three groups, and give each group a copy of the text and the following instructions. Give the groups about 20 minutes to complete the task.

---

**A VAK experiment**

**Group V: Visual**
The text is for a coursebook for students of English. Your job is to provide some visual support to help students understand the text and the vocabulary in it. You can draw pictures, diagrams, maps (or download pictures from google images if you have a computer available). Make a poster to illustrate your ideas. You can cut the text and put it in the middle of the poster if you wish.

**Group A: Auditory**
The text is for a coursebook for students of English. Your job is to make a good recording of it so that students can listen to it, as well as read it. Decide how you will record it and rehearse. Your teacher will help you with pronunciation. Prepare a recording and, if you can, record it.

**Group K: Kinaesthetic**
Your job is to create some mime and action to accompany the story, to help people understand the text and the vocabulary in it. Prepare to perform the story.

---

### Step Three
- Group V present their poster to the rest of the class.
- Group A play their recording or read the text aloud.
- Group K perform their mimes/actions while Group A are performing.

### Step Four
The students discuss in groups of three (V+A+K in each group) the three ways of working, and which they preferred.

### Step Five
Round off with whole-class feedback. You could repeat the activity another day with a different text and the groups taking a different letter.

# The black book

## Keeping a record of students' mistakes

### Rationale
This activity will help you to listen carefully to your learners and be more sensitive to their difficulties in speaking English.

### Activity
You keep a systematic note of your learners' mistakes for one week, for use in future classes.

---

### Step One
Buy a notebook (A4 or A5 size). It doesn't have to be black! Assign a page for each lesson you are teaching the following week. You can do this chronologically, or grouped by class or level. Divide each page into four columns (or quarters, as in the example Pro-forma below).

### Step Two
In each lesson, and for one week, make notes in the book, on the appropriate page and in the appropriate place, when the students are doing a speaking activity.

### Step Three
At the end of the week, read through the book.

### Step Four
Choose one of these three options:
- Use the notes you have made as a kind of mini-syllabus for future teaching of language points.
- Photocopy a page (or pages) from the book and give it to your students to discuss and correct.
- Write a text or dialogue containing the mistakes and ask the students to correct it.

You may choose to hand the black book over to a student for a lesson and let them keep a record of the errors and successes they notice.

---

**Keeping a record**

| Grammar/Vocabulary | Pronunciation |
|---|---|
| *I go always to cinema.* | *Comfort__able__* |
| *She have got a cat.* | *Bag – said 'back'* |
| *Does she can swim?* | *Intonation very flat in 'Can I help you?'* |
| *Swimming bath* | |
| *My fathers* | |
| **Use of L1** | **Very good English** |
| *Bodega* | *I don't ever see my sister.* |
| *Ocio* | *Have you seen Quantum of Solace?* |
| *¿Yo qué sé?* | *Good pronunciation of 'amazing'* |

# Ready, steady, record!

## Playing back for future planning

### Rationale

This is a very simple idea and it is not new, but it is immensely useful for teachers and students. You will have the time to analyse their performance in more depth than in class, and your students will become more aware of their English. The procedure here is designed to make it as easy as possible to carry out. There are two versions, according to resources you have available.

### Activity

You record your students speaking then play the recording back, so that they and you can both hear how they perform.

 **1  If most of your students have MP3s.**

### Step One

Tell the students to bring their MP3 players to class. These usually have built-in microphones. You will need one per pair, so it doesn't matter if some forget. If you have fewer than half the students with an MP3, do a second speaking activity and pass the MP3 recorders round.

### Step Two

Set the students a short speaking task to do in pairs and tell them, when they are ready, to record themselves. For example, ask them to talk about two cities they know and to say which they prefer.

### Step Three

The students listen to their conversations in their pairs, using their headphones (one ear-piece each). They can repeat the activity and make a second recording if they wish. They usually want to improve, and it is good to encourage this, although you need to set a time limit.

### Step Four

Ask for a copy of the files. These can either be transferred onto your or the school's computer, or the students can send you the file as an e-mail attachment.

### Step Five

Listen to the recordings after class. Make notes on difficulties the students had. You can use the following catagories:

- Grammar
- Vocabulary
- Pronunciation
- Use of L1

Use a Pro-forma like the one opposite to organise your notes: the information will help you plan future classes. Note examples of successful usage. too.

| Recording students' performance | |
| --- | --- |
| **Grammar/Vocabulary** | **Pronunciation** |
| *Is more big.* | *Important* |
| *There are too much cars.* | *'Poluthion'* (for pollution) |
| *Did you was there?* | *The weather was very bad.* (stress!) |
| *The people are sympatic.* | *Walk v work* |
| *Is very pollution.* | |
| **Use of L1** | **Very good English** |
| *Acera* | *I wouldn't recommend it.* |
| *Museo* | *There is a lot more to do in Barcelona.* |
| *Ladrón* | *The nightlife in Madrid is better.* |
| *¿Qué dices?* | |

 **2  If your students don't have MP3s, you will need an MP3/dictaphone/tape recorder with microphone.**

### Step One

Have a set of speaking prompts prepared. (For example: 'talk about your brother or sister', 'discuss the weather', 'tell your partner about a film you have seen recently'.) You need one prompt for every two students.

### Step Two

Pair the students, and give each pair a prompt. Tell them to talk for about two minutes. Record one of the pairs.

### Step Three

Repeat until you have recorded all the pairs.

If you have more than eight students, you might want to spread this over two or three lessons, recording just four pairs per lesson. Alternatively, in a large class, you can ask for three or four volunteer pairs to record.

### Step Four

Play the recordings to the class. (You can always leave this stage out, depending on how you think the students will feel about it.)

### Step Five

Listen to the recordings after class. Make notes on the difficulties the students had. Use the Pro-forma above to help organise your notes: the information will help you plan future classes.

### Variation

The students can be given the Pro-formas to correct themselves when they listen back.

# Teaching back to front

## Varying the arrangement of the room

### Rationale

'Psychogeography' refers to the way seating arrangements and positioning can affect communication. This activity encourages you to play with this, and observe the effects it can have in your classroom. It can be as simple as you standing at the back of the classroom rather than at the front.

### Activity

Trying out new seating arrangements in your classroom.

### Step One

In the diagram opposite, there are ten examples of classroom layouts for students. Look at the list of typical classroom activities below and decide which layouts could be appropriate. Be creative. Think of at least two possible layouts for each activity type.

**Classroom activities**

| | Layout |
|---|---|
| Discussion/debate | |
| Roleplay in closed pairs | |
| Teacher presenting grammar or vocabulary | |
| Drilling | |
| Listening to a recording | |
| Watching a DVD | |
| Reading | |
| Writing, with teacher correcting | |
| Peer dictation | |
| Practising speaking on the telephone | |
| Doing written exercises with other students | |
| Free speaking with a partner | |
| Project work | |
| Playing a game | |
| Speaking with lots of other students | |
| Listening to a teacher anecdote | |
| Performing a roleplay to the class | |
| Practising reading a dialogue with a partner | |
| Doing written exercises alone | |
| Doing a class survey | |

### Step Two

Choose a layout which you don't normally use and choose an activity in one of your classes to use it for. For example, if your students are normally in a horseshoe for pairwork practice (layout 1), try a wheel (layout 4).

**Classroom layouts**

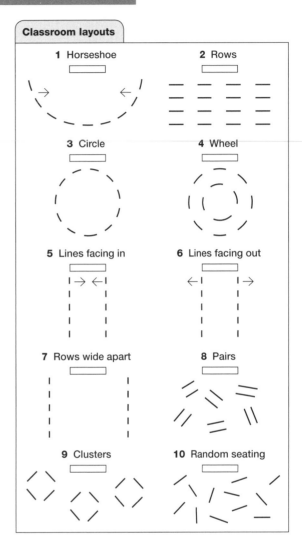

1 Horseshoe
2 Rows
3 Circle
4 Wheel
5 Lines facing in
6 Lines facing out
7 Rows wide apart
8 Pairs
9 Clusters
10 Random seating

### Step Three

When you come to do the activity in class, tell the students you want *them* to move the chairs. Draw what you want on the board, to help them.

### Step Four

The students do the activity.

### Step Five

After the activity, get a quick reaction from the students. How did the layout change the way they worked or the way they felt? Having done this activity, you may want to use more variations of classroom layout in the future.

### Variation

Try any of these seating arrangements standing up.

# Teaching inside out
## Using mother-tongue materials to practise English

### Rationale
L1 materials such as songs and newspaper articles are easy to find, relevant to students and can generate very useful language work, as students start on the inside, with their own language, and turn it into the target language.

### Activity
In a monolingual class, you teach English using an item of mother-tongue input as the basis for your class activity.

### Step One
You (or your students) choose an L1 text: a song, an article from a newspaper or magazine, or from the internet. Consider the English your students will need in order to deal with the material and the possible help you will need to give them.

### Step Two
Prepare the activity. Here are some ideas:

- Give the students two minutes to skim read the text. Then one student turns it over and gives a summary of the text in English to another, who checks, corrects and clarifies any problems.
- Alternatively, the student with the text asks questions to the student who has turned it over. Both questions and answers should be in English.
- The students translate the first 50 words on their own in writing. They then compare.
- Turn the text into a listening task. Read out a translation of the text, but include a few factual mistakes. Then give out the L1 texts, and the students read to see if they can spot the errors.
- Give the texts out. The students work alone and choose five words or phrases they would like to know the English for. They then work with a partner and compare words and phrases, peer teaching each other the translation where possible. They must make a new list of five remaining words or phrases. Repeat this process with pairs joining pairs.

Encourage the students to ask questions like: *How do you say 'X' in English?* Be prepared to offer help, but avoid overpreparing support materials. Let the students do the work, and simply be prepared to respond to requests for help.

### Step Three
When you have carried out the activity, you and your students can complete the two prompts below and discuss:

- This activity was good because ...
- This activity was difficult because ...

This will help you and them to understand the advantages and disadvantages of using material from their mother tongue.

# Teaching in reverse
## Teacher-student role reversal

### Rationale
Exchanging roles can be very empowering for students and enlightening for teachers. It is often funny, too, which is probably why it is a popular device in several Hollywood films.

### Activity
You exchange roles with a student.

### Step One
If your students are familiar with Hollywood films, you can set the scene with a brief discussion of *Big, Freaky Friday*, or other role-reversal films.

### Step Two
Set up a speaking activity. For example, the students work in pairs or small groups to discuss their plans for the weekend.

### Step Three
Ask for a volunteer to exchange roles with you for five minutes (or draw names from a hat to choose who it is). Sit down in the student's seat and invite the student to sit in yours or stand where you usually stand. Give the student your board pen. You can brief them on what to do if you feel it necessary.

### Step Four
Continue the class. The students do the speaking activity with you, the teacher, as one of the students, and the new 'teacher' monitoring, correcting, etc.

### Step Five
After the activity, ask the student-teacher to continue in the role, if you feel they would like to, conducting feedback, nominating students to report back, correcting their English, offering praise, and so on.

### Step Six
Return to your original roles. Get the class to give the student-teacher a round of applause.

# Teaching upside down

## Trying a completely new method

### Rationale

Trying out a new method, and turning your regular teaching routine on its head, can give you important insights into your own method of teaching. Your students will enjoy the change and learn from the experience. It may open up a discussion about methods in general. In this activity you experiment with Community Language Learning (CLL*).

### Activity

You teach a lesson using Community Language Learning (in a monolingual class – the other methods suggested are more open).

### Note

You need to be able to speak your students' L1 to do this. The activity works best with elementary-level students. You need a small group (maximum eight students). If you have more, you can designate extra students as 'substitutes' and have them change places with the starting eight as the lesson progresses. Also, you need to record students in this activity.

### Step One

Tell the students they are going to be sampling a new method. Tell them the activity will take 20 minutes.

### Step Two

The eight students and you sit in a circle, with a recording device at the ready.

### Step Three

Tell the students they are going to have a conversation in English about anything they want. You will help them by translating what they want to say (or just the items they don't know in English) from their mother tongue into English, and by helping them with pronunciation. They will record the conversation.

### Step Four

The conversation begins, with a student raising their hand and telling you in their L1 what they want to say. For example:
*'I want to ask Pablo if he saw the match last night.'*
You, the teacher, supply the English version and, if necessary, drill it. Then the student addresses the question to Pablo:
*'Did you see the match last night?'*
The question is recorded.

### Step Five

Pablo replies, and the conversation continues in this way, with other students joining in, for about 10-15 minutes.

### Step Six

Play the recording of the conversation to the students, and work further on the language/pronunciation if you wish.

### Step Seven

Discuss with the students how they felt about learning English this way.
- What are the pros and cons?
- Would they like to repeat the experience?
Are there elements of the new method they found particularly helpful which you could incorporate in your usual class?

*__Community Language Learning__ is an approach in which students work together to develop what aspects of a language they would like to learn. The teacher acts as a counsellor and a paraphraser, while the learner acts as a collaborator. The method was developed by Charles A. Curran, a professor of psychology at Loyola University, USA. It is also known as 'Counselling Learning', as Curran likened the teacher-student relationship to that of counsellor and client.

## Multiple methods

If you want to experiment some more with *teaching upside down*, there are many other methods which you might like to try with your students.
- You can keyword search on the internet for more information.
- For detailed descriptions of how these methods work in class, you can consult *Techniques and Principles in Language Teaching* by Diane Larsen-Freeman (OUP 2000).

### The Silent Way

The teacher says very little. The method entails a good deal of eliciting from students, who put sounds together from visual clues. The teacher uses gesture to create meaning and context.

### Suggestopædia

A relaxing and inspiring environment is created with comfortable chairs and music. The students read and 'absorb' language from texts in the target language, and translation is also used.

### Audio-lingual Method

Based on behaviourist psychology, which views language learning as habit formation. The method entails mainly 'listen and repeat' activities, with dialogues and drills and strictly no use of the mother tongue.

### Total Physical Response

Based on students listening to and following instructions given by the teacher. It resembles the way we learn our first language: through listening to parents and responding with physical movement.

# You and your colleagues

## The third circle

In the first two circles, we looked at development activities you can do alone and with your students. We are now in the third circle, where the activities incorporate other teachers, sometimes *with* your students and sometimes *without*. These activities can be more difficult to set up, given that they require more negotiation and co-operation, as we move from independent to co-dependent action. On the other hand, they can be very satisfying and rewarding for this same reason.

Development activities with your colleagues work mainly on the S and E motivations in the RISE model (see the introduction to the first circle and the activity on page 22): Self-improvement and Enjoyment. However, as they are by nature more 'public' activities, you may also gain Recognition.

Opposite is a checklist of things you can do in collaboration with your fellow teachers to develop yourself and your teaching. Which things are of particular interest to you? Which have you already done? Which have you not thought of doing? Which might you like to concentrate on? Read through the list and give yourself a score for each item.

There are two fundamental places where developmental collaboration can occur with colleagues: inside the classroom, with your students, and in the staffroom (in other words: outside the classroom). However, some activity, like mentoring, will move between the two, and will take place 'in and out'.

### In the classroom

Peer observation, in various forms, and team teaching (teaching a class together) are two key ways for teachers to develop their awareness of their own teaching. One problem with peer observation can be the interpretation of the role of the observer. Despite the best intentions, observers can often find themselves being critical and judgemental, perhaps because this is the model they are familiar with, as a consequence of evaluative observations on training courses and from employers. The effectiveness of peer observation as a developmental, rather than evaluative, tool depends on:

- the relationship between you and your colleague;
- how you structure the activity;
- the ability of you both to communicate clearly and with sensitivity;
- taking care with the use of judgemental feedback.

The activities in this section are structured to encourage teachers to share classrooms in a non-evaluative way, or with evaluation strictly controlled by the observee. In

---

**Personal checklist**

There are things you can do with your colleagues to develop yourself and your teaching. Read down the list.

- Give yourself a score from 0-5 for each item, according to how often you do it (0 = 'never done this', 5 = 'done this a lot').
- Then complete the right-hand column, adding a tick (✔) where appropriate, if you would like to try something, or do more of it

| Things I have done (or not done) ... | Score (0-5) | (✔) |
|---|---|---|
| Discussed TEFL theory/literature with a colleague | | |
| Observed a colleague | | |
| Been observed by a colleague | | |
| Swapped materials | | |
| Shared the teaching of a lesson with a colleague | | |
| Videoed myself teaching | | |
| Acted as mentor or mentee | | |
| Spent time socially with colleagues | | |
| Taken part in team-building activities with colleagues | | |
| Set up a blog, wiki or web project with colleagues | | |

**Comment**
Looking at this list should help identify areas of particular interest for you (or that you hadn't perhaps thought of) and will help you decide which activities you would most like to do.

---

other words, they are activities for *development* rather than *training*. And there are certainly plenty of areas that you can focus on, both general, regarding your way of teaching, and specific, regarding a particular class. These areas can cover multiple aspects of your teaching:

- Language – how you correct students or how you explain or clarify new language.
- Classroom routines – how you give instructions, use the whiteboard, or how much time you talk.
- Classroom management – your responses to disruptive behaviour, and how you control your students' reactions and their performance in activities.
- Rapport – your body language and movement, and your interactions with individual students.

The activity *Be my judge* does allow for more judgemental comment from a colleague, but in a well-defined framework, and it focuses on three of these areas. *Scary Movie* is perhaps especially helpful for looking at aspects of your teaching such as your body language and your 'teacher talk'.

So how can we ensure that we receive the information we want, in order to be able to act upon it, without feeling 'under attack'? Below are some suggestions on how to communicate effectively with colleagues when conducting peer observations.

**Observers** should:
- allow the observee to control the situation;
- ask the observee what they would like them to observe exactly, and follow their instructions;
- say, if asked to give feedback, three positive things for every 'suggestion' they wish to make.

**Observees** should:
- control the situation;
- give the observer some specific instructions about what they would like them to observe;
- elicit as much or as little feedback as *they* want.

**Both of you** should:
- mind your language;
- describe rather than evaluate;
- listen carefully.

If you are interested in working more on your communication skills, you can try the activity *Six ways of talking*, in circle five. Opposite here are some guidelines on what to do and what not to do (and say), when collaborating with other teachers.

## In the staffroom
The staffroom (both as a place and as a collection of colleagues) can be a key factor in your development as a teacher. The atmosphere in the staffroom, and the relationships you form with colleagues, can provide the confidence, support and motivation to inspire development. The activities in this section are aimed at helping you to create and maintain a positive staffroom atmosphere and to build rapport with your colleagues. They cover collaborative projects, bonding, discreet observation and trialling activities.

And for teachers who work off-site or don't have a staffroom to gather in, the best way to stay in contact with colleagues and build a sense of community is online. This can be done through the use of blogs, or tools such as Facebook and Moodle, which provide a space for teachers to store information and exchange ideas. The final activity in this section, *Virtual staffroom*, deals with this.

## In and out
The two 'mentoring' activities in this section involve working with a colleague both inside and outside the classroom. A mentor is a (usually experienced) person who gives support to the growth and learning of another person (usually

| **Observation** | | |
| **Observers do say…** | **Observers don't say…** | **Recommendations** |
| --- | --- | --- |
| *Two of the pairs were speaking in Spanish in the second practice activity.* | *There's lots of Spanish spoken in your class.* | Be objective rather than subjective when describing the lesson. Avoid generalising. |
| *I noticed some students weren't sure what they had to do.* | *Your instructions weren't clear.* | Focus on outcomes rather than making judgements. |
| *There was…* | *You should have…* | Remember that description is better than prescription. |
| *I enjoyed your lesson / I got a really useful idea from your lesson.* | *That was a really good lesson.* | Avoid evaluating the lesson. Make any judgements subjective. |
| *You could…* | *What I always do in these situations is…* | Be helpful, avoiding the message 'I am a better teacher than you'. |
| *Students arrived late… I often wonder what to do in these situations.* | *Students arrived late… but that wasn't your fault.* | Encourage your colleague to find solutions rather than excuses. |

less experienced), to help them integrate in a specific community. Because mentoring is a relationship-based activity, it can have significant impact on development for both the mentee or the mentor. *Standing in the shadow* focuses on the mentee role, and *Mentor for a month* on the mentor role.

These activities have concentrated on developing atmosphere and relationships, through informal collaborations with colleagues.

More formal interactions are dealt with in the next circle, where we take one step further, building on this collaboration with colleagues to incorporate activities which involve the school management as well as fellow teachers in an institutional setting.

# Be my guest

## A colleague visits your class

### Rationale

Inviting a colleague to come to your class as a guest provides an informal context to see each other interacting with students. It also provides some variety and fun for your students! This is a good activity to do if you have a problem class or problem student and you would like to introduce a discreet 'second set of eyes and ears' into your classroom.

### Activity

A fellow teacher participates in your class as a guest.

**Step One**

Find a colleague to do this activity with.

**Step Two**

Tell your colleague you would like them to make a guest appearance in your class and agree what form this could take. Here are some suggestions:

- Chat show – you interview them about their job, their life in general, or something specific, like a hobby or a trip they have been on.
- Press conference – the students interview them about any of the above.
- Mini-talk – your colleague gives a five-minute presentation, followed by questions from you and the students.

**Step Three**

Agree a time to do this when your colleague is free. Agree a duration for the activity, for example 20 minutes.

**Step Four**

On the day, introduce your colleague to your students and carry out the activity. For a press conference and mini-talk, you can take the role of 'language resource' for your learners, helping them to formulate questions and clarifying difficult language.

**Step Five**

After the class, discuss with your colleague their impressions of your students - their use of English and their motivation, for example. If you have a problem student or students, you can discuss them with your colleague and consider possible causes and lines of action.

**Step Six**

Carry out any actions that emerged as potentially beneficial, both for you and your students, and offer to do the same for your colleague, inviting them to choose the form of *your* 'appearance' in *their* class.

# Be my student

## A teacher joins your class as a learner

### Rationale

Having a colleague participate in your class as a student and then feed back to you helps you to become more aware of how your students experience the lesson.

### Activity

A fellow teacher participates in your class as one of your students, helping you and helping them in the process

**Step One**

Find a colleague to do this activity with. This should be a colleague who you trust and respect.

**Step Two**

Tell them you would like them to participate in your class as a student, and agree a time to do this when your colleague is free.

**Step Three**

At the start of the lesson, introduce the colleague to your students. Explain that they will be joining the class as a 'very advanced student'. They will participate in all the activities, sometimes helping their 'fellow students' when they have the opportunity, in pair- and groupwork for example. They will also be getting homework!

**Step Four**

Teach the class as you would normally, treating your colleague exactly as you do the other students. Encourage the colleague to 'peer teach' where useful. Create humour where possible, too, for example by correcting their pronunciation!

**Step Five**

After the class, ask your colleague for some feedback on their experience as a student in your class (see the suggestions on colleague/observer feedback in the introduction to this circle).

**Step Six**

Homework! Ask your colleague to write and e-mail to you a short 'learner diary entry' for the class, describing the experience.

## Be my judge

### A colleague observes your class and gives you feedback

### Rationale

Your colleague will hear and notice things which you can't. In addition to noting objectively what happened, judgemental comments can be helpful as long as you limit and define their scope.

### Activity

A fellow teacher observes your class and makes notes and judgemental comments on an aspect of your teaching chosen by you.

### Step One

Choose an aspect of your teaching that you feel you would like to improve or understand better. The topic can be a general one which applies to all your classes, or a specific one about a particular class you teach. The examples opposite are related to:
- Discipline problems
- How you give instructions
- Your use of the whiteboard

### Step Two

Find a colleague to do this activity with. This should be a colleague who you trust and respect.

### Step Three

Tell them you would like them to help you understand better a certain aspect of your teaching. You would like them to observe your class and make notes, *but only on this aspect*, and afterwards discuss their notes with you. It can be useful to devise a Pro-forma for your colleague to use, like those opposite, which have been filled in to illustrate how they might work.

### Step Four

Agree a time to do this when your colleague is free.

### Step Five

At the start of the lesson, introduce your colleague to your students. Explain that they will be observing the class to help you understand your teaching better. Make it clear they will not be assessing the students in any way.

### Step Six

Teach the class.

### Step Seven

After the class, read and discuss the notes your colleague has made.

### Step Eight

Offer to do the same for your colleague. If you are the observer, think carefully about how you will express yourself. See the introduction to this circle, for some suggestions.

**Disruptive behaviour**

| Description of incident | What the teacher did | How the students reacted | Observer's comments |
|---|---|---|---|
| Violeta and Karina talking while you were addressing the group. | Said sharply and in a raised voice: 'Violeta, can you stop talking and listen?' | They stopped talking. | Why did you only address Violeta? |

**Instructions**

| Description of the instructions | Time taken | How the students carried out the task | Observer's suggestions for improvement |
|---|---|---|---|
| You explained the task and did an example with one student. You asked if everyone understood. | 4 mins. | One pair put their hands up and asked you to explain to them again. The other pairs did the activity as you wanted, except one pair who wrote the dialogue instead of speaking. | Make it clear whether you want students to speak or write. Check understanding of task by asking a random student: 'What do you have to do?' |

**Whiteboard**

**Instructions to the observer:** Draw illustrations (or take photos) of the whiteboard at different stages of the lesson, and make comments in the spaces provided.

Feb 24th.

It's something you use for ...

You can _____ with it.

Drying
Cutting
Sharpening

hammer
nail
scissors
hair-dryer
cardboard
saw
pencil-sharpener
ironing-board

**Observer's comments:**
*The picture of the hammer and nail is very clear.*
*You could illustrate the form: 'something you use for cutting paper'.*
*You erased the vocabulary. Leave it for reference?*

# All change!

### Planning and teaching someone else's lesson

### Rationale

This activity will help you to see your students and your coursebook from a different perspective. The process of writing out a lesson plan for a colleague to teach and the reverse – having to teach to a plan your colleague has written for you – helps you to understand your own teaching better.

### Activity

You and a colleague plan a lesson for each other. This activity requires about an hour to do, as it involves writing a lesson plan in a more detailed way than you would normally do.

### Step One

Find a colleague to do the activity with.

### Step Two

Choose a class, or part of a class, you would like your colleague to prepare for you (about 30 minutes to one hour). Ask them to do the same for you.

### Step Three

Brief each other about the class (in person or via e-mail). Include information on the following:

- The level of the students
- Where they are in the coursebook
- The types of activity they enjoy
- What you would like the lesson to cover (this can be specific: 'page 45, ex. 1–4', or vague: 'vocabulary and speaking on the theme of transport'.

### Step Four

Write a plan for each other, based on the briefing. Here are some tips for writing the plan:

- Make the aims clear.
- Make the steps clear.
- Don't include too much detail – one page of A4 maximum.

### Step Five

Exchange plans with your colleague and clarify understanding, as necessary.

### Step Six

You do the class as your colleague has planned for you. They do the class you have planned for them.

### Step Seven

Exchange feedback on what you learnt from the experience. For example, you could tell your colleague:

- one thing which you learnt from their way of planning;
- the part of the plan which you thought worked best.

# Dream team

### You and a colleague teach a class together

### Rationale

Sharing preparation and teaching allows you and your colleague to bond and learn from each other through collaboration. It also provides an interesting change for your students.

### Activity

You prepare and teach a class together with a colleague.

### Step One

Find a colleague to work with. You are A and B. Decide on a class you are going to team teach. It can be a class of either of you.

### Step Two

Teacher A , the regular teacher of the class, plans the lesson.

### Step Three

Teacher B looks at the plan and allocates who will lead which stages of the lesson and the role of the other teacher in those stages (Spectator, Participant, Model). For example:

- Teacher A gives the instructions for a speaking activity. Teacher B watches. (Spectator)
- Teachers A and B demonstrate the activity for the students together. (Model)
- Finally, as the students do the activity, Teacher B joins in the activity (Participant) while Teacher A circulates and notes down language problems the students have.

Aim to allocate a good balance of the SPM roles.

### Step Four

Teach the class together, as you have planned.

### Step Five

Discuss the experience briefly and informally with your colleague after the class.

## Scary Movie

### Someone videos you teaching

### Rationale

This is one of the simplest and most effective ways to help you reflect on your teaching, and develop as a result. Teachers often fear this procedure, perhaps feeling anxious about how they look on camera more than about their teaching!

### Activity

A colleague or friend videos you teaching.

### Step One

Before you start, read the tips in the box below.

> **Teaching on film**
>
> - Take charge of the procedure. You tell the cameraperson what you want them to film and when.
> - Don't film everything: 20 minutes in total is enough. This can be a 20-minute chunk, or short takes, at different points of the lesson.
> - Film the students doing activities with you monitoring, not just you at the front of the class.
> - Watch the video after class, on your own if you prefer. Don't feel obliged to let others watch with you.
> - Brush your hair and wear something nice.

### Step Two

Find a video camera and someone to operate it. This needn't be another teacher. It can be a friend or administrative colleague. The person needn't be skilled in any way, but they will need:

- to know how the camera works (on/off, zoom);
- to be given an idea of what you want them to film.

### Step Three

Choose a room to film in, if possible one which is small and has carpet, as this will give better sound. Arrange the room so that the cameraperson can move easily. If the camera works from the mains, make sure the cable is long enough to move around with, or arrange the class to be within view from a fixed position.

### Step Four

At the start of the lesson, explain to the students that you will be filming parts of the lesson to help you learn about your teaching. Help them to relax, perhaps with a few jokes.

### Step Five

Teach the lesson, while your colleague films.

### Step Six

Watch the video. You may want to do this several times, as you will start to notice different things each time you watch.

## Sharing board

### Pooling material with colleagues

### Rationale

Sharing material and ideas often takes place naturally. The sharing board allows this to be done more systematically and reach more teachers. It is a place where teachers can attach something they would really like to share with colleagues. For example:

- Material they have made
- A description of a good activity they have used
- A photocopy of an interesting activity they have found in a book or on the internet

### Activity

Creating a space in the staffroom where teachers can pin up materials and lesson ideas to share.

### Step One

Prepare a sharing board in your staffroom. If you have an existing notice board you can create a space on it. If you don't, you can create a sharing board by simply sticking a large rectangle of coloured paper on the wall with the title 'Sharing Board'.

### Step Two

Put up the rules for using the sharing board next to it. You may want to add further rules of your own to the ones suggested here.

> **Sharing Board – Rules for Use**
>
> - Post one idea at a time.
> - Leave space for others.
> - Put your name on the material, or near it so that people will know who posted it.
> - If you post something, make sure it is clear how to use it.
> - If you use something, thank the person who posted it.

### Step Three

Start by putting up on the board something you would like to share with your colleagues. Encourage a colleague to do the same, so there are already two activities on the board for others to use and as examples to follow.

### Step Four

Manage the board. When it gets full, start removing the oldest activities to create space for new ones.

# Book club

## A jigsaw reading project for teachers

### Rationale

Reading and reporting back to colleagues is motivating because it is interactive and because it entails an element of responsibility. If you are expected to report on a book, you are more likely to read it.

### Activity

You read and report back on an ELT book and find out about two others.

### Step One

Find two colleagues to do this activity with.

### Step Two

Each person chooses an ELT book to read or browse, one which they haven't read or have hardly read. It can be an activity book or a more theoretical book from the shelf of your staffroom, from the library, or from a bookshop if you have some money to spend.

### Step Three

Agree a deadline with your two colleagues for finishing the task. Somewhere around two weeks may be suitable. Arrange to meet for an hour, to report back on what you have read. Enter the appointment in your diary.

### Step Four

Read/browse the book and make notes. Use the Pro-forma below, and make copies for your colleagues if they wish.

| Book club project | |
|---|---|
| Name of the book: | |
| What type of book is it? | |
| What does it contain? | |
| Examples of interesting ideas in the book: | |
| Examples of useful activities in the book: | |

### Step Five

Meet for one hour and report back to each other on the books you have read. Spend 20 minutes on each book. You all use your notes to help you remember what you want to say.

### Variation

Instead of a book, you can choose a professional magazine or website for language teachers or learners.

# Try before you buy

## Testing a teaching activity with a colleague

### Rationale

This activity will help you with your lesson planning. You find out if an activity works, how it works and what language your students will require to carry it out.

### Activity

You trial a speaking activity you intend for your students with a colleague first.

### Step One

Find a colleague who is willing to help you.

### Step Two

Do the speaking activity you are planning to give your students with your colleague, exactly as you plan to do it. For example: if the activity is *'compare two cities you know well, using the following prompts…'*, then do exactly that with your colleague. You can record the conversation if you want to.

### Step Three

When you have finished, consider the following:
- Any difficulties you had thinking of things to say
- How much time you needed
- Whether you needed any preparation
- Whether your students would have enough English to do the task
- If the activity is intended to practise a particular language point, did this language in fact get used by you and your colleague?

### Step Four

Use your reflections from Step Three to adapt the activity and how you set it up. For example, you may find you need to pre-teach students some key vocabulary. Or you may find that the target language you are aiming for doesn't arise and you need to adapt the activity or the instructions, or even replace it with another one

# Fly on the wall

## Listening to staffroom talk

### Rationale

What we talk about in the staffroom, and how we talk about it, says a lot about the place where we work and our attitudes as teachers. This task is intended to be light-hearted, nonetheless it will be thought-provoking and may cause change.

### Activity

You listen and make a record of what you and your colleagues talk about in the staffroom.

### Step One

For one week, listen to conversations in your staffroom and note down the categories they fall into, using the Pro-forma below. In some cases, you will mark two categories, for example if you hear a conversation where someone is complaining about a student. Do this discreetly, so that your colleagues don't notice.

Here is an example of how your sheet might look at the end of the week:

| Staffroom talk | |
|---|---|
| Talk about school administration | I I I I |
| Talk about teaching | I I I |
| Talk about students | I I I I I I |
| Complaining | I I I I I I I |
| Celebrating | I I I |
| Talk about life outside the school | I I I I I I I I I I I I I I |
| Talk about colleagues | I I |
| Talk about management | I I I I |

### Step Two

When the week is over, post your sheet on the noticeboard with an explanation of your 'research'.

### Step Three

Provoke some (light-hearted) discussion on how you and your colleagues talk in the staffroom and what that says about you as a group.

# The name is bond

## A five-minute rapport-building crossword

### Rationale

Doing an activity together encourages bonding. This activity may get teachers from different sub-groups in the staffroom to come together.

### Activity

You complete a crossword with colleagues. This activity works well with two to five teachers.

### Step One

Photocopy a simple crossword (from a book or newspaper) and pin it up in the staffroom during a break. Invite anyone interested to complete it with you. When you have assembled a few colleagues, nominate one of them to write the answers.

### Step Two

Do the crossword as quickly as possible (or as much as you can in five minutes) as a team, with one person writing and the others calling out the answers.

### Step Three

Repeat the activity on a daily or weekly basis, aiming to beat your best performance.

### Step Four

Try some more bonding activities, particularly if the first one proved successful.

| Basic bonding activities |
|---|
| **Brain teasers**<br>Post a brain teaser or lateral-thinking problem on the board in the staffroom. This will encourage discussion during the day. Post the answer at the end of the day. |
| **Self-diagnostic tests**<br>Tests on themes such as leadership, multiple intelligences, personality type, learning style, and so on, can be found on the internet. In many cases, they offer a print-out with results, sometimes in a light-hearted style. Find a test and post *your* result. Encourage your colleagues to do the same and read each other's. |
| **Food and drink**<br>Bring in some food or drink to share. In some cultures, this is done for someone's birthday, but it is a simple and effective way of boosting togetherness at any time. Avoid the temptation to over-organise this with a rota or 'biscuit club'. It works best as a spontaneous gesture. |
| **'Top six' lists**<br>Post a top six list on the noticeboard: your top six films, top six local restaurants, top six games for teaching, etc. Invite other teachers to do the same and start new lists of their own. These lists provide an interesting focus for discussion and source of useful information. |

# Virtual staffroom
## Online communication with colleagues

### Rationale

Even if you are in regular face-to-face contact with colleagues, there are good reasons to build an online staffroom:

- Teachers can keep in touch easily when they are away from school.
- Some people communicate more effectively in written form.
- You can share materials, ideas and links to useful websites easily and 'paper free'.

### Activity

You create a virtual space online for staff to communicate with each other.

---

### Step One

Create a blog* at www.blogger.com. A blog is a mini web-page. It is very simple to create and use, and is free.

### Step Two

Get people to visit the blog by posting something:

- very interesting (gossip, news);
- very useful (teaching links, a lesson plan, materials);
- very essential (a map of how to get to a party).

Don't worry if the blog takes a while to get going or has some periods of relative inactivity. This is quite normal.

### Step Three

Use your blog to do the following:

- Write messages to other teachers
- Debate and exchange views on a particular subject
- Share teaching materials such as hand outs, sound files and pictures
- Share links to interesting sites

### Step Four

Outwards and onwards. If your blog is successful, you may want to link up with other schools. You could use the blog to create a link with a school in another country, for example.

*You can also create a virtual staffroom using a Wiki, MySpace or Moodle.

# Standing in the shadow
## Being with a mentor for a day

### Rationale

This is a kind of extended peer observation, or 'reduced mentoring' activity. The advantage of spending the day shadowing an experienced colleague is that you learn more about how they deal with the challenges of the day inside and outside class time. You also grow to understand your colleague better.

### Activity

You spend a day with an experienced teacher (or a half-day if that is easier).

---

### Step One

Choose a 'mentor type' colleague, one who you think you can learn from.

### Step Two

Ask the mentor if you can shadow them for a day. Being a shadow means spending the whole time by someone's side (well, nearly the whole time): when they prepare, when they teach, when they relax between lessons.

### Step Three

Arrange a suitable day for your shadowing.

### Step Four

Spend as much time together as is practically possible:

- Accompany your mentor to all their classes and observe unobtrusively.
- Spend some time outside class with them while they are preparing. Offer to help.
- Chat with your mentor between lessons about the lessons and the students in general.

### Step Five

Send your mentor a follow-up e-mail, thanking them and saying what you gained from the experience of standing in their shadow. This will consolidate developmental benefits for them, as well as for you.

# Mentor for a month

## Mentoring a colleague over a period of time

### Rationale

Helping a new teacher adjust to working in your school and possibly to cultural challenges (coming from another country, for example, or a school with a completely different system) can be rewarding in itself and a useful contribution to your school, as well as to your own development.

### Activity

You mentor a new teacher for one month.

### Step One

Write an e-mail to your director of studies, explaining you would like to volunteer to mentor a new teacher. Include an explanation of the benefits for the teacher, for the school and for you. Say why you think you would make a good mentor.

### Step Two

Arrange to meet to discuss who you will mentor and how. Your mentee should be someone who:

- will benefit from the mentor-mentee relationship;
- you can establish trust and rapport with;
- is eager to learn;
- has a positive attitude to learning through a mentor relationship.

Remember that mentor-mentee relationships can work very well with people who are different in terms of age, gender, attitudes and interests – not necessarily someone just like you.

### Step Three

With your mentee, decide on the objectives of the scheme and write these down. Here are some suggestions:

**For the mentee:**

- To feel they have had the necessary support to teach effectively in the early stages of the new job.
- To feel happy and well settled in the school (and the culture, if this is new).
- To feel they have benefitted from the mentor's help.
- To feel they can continue to teach effectively and develop *after* the mentoring has finished.

**For the mentor:**

- To feel the positive effects of the mentoring and how they might improve as a mentor next time.

**For the school:**

- To feel that the mentee has adapted better to the job as a result of the scheme, and to recognise the contribution of the mentor.

### Step Four

Decide with your mentee what to include in your mentoring scheme, and why. A checklist of possible elements is suggested here, and you can obviously add your own.

| With mentoring in mind | |
| --- | --- |
| Mentor observes mentee. | |
| Mentee observes mentor. | |
| Mentor co-teaches with mentee for one class or part of a class. | |
| Mentor gives mentee a guided tour of the teaching resources in the school. | |
| Mentee explains the school administration procedures. | |
| Mentee shares inside knowledge of the school 'culture' (who's who, typical issues at the school, school policy, school philosophy, etc). | |
| Mentor introduces mentee to the other staff at work and socially. | |
| Mentor helps mentee to plan lessons. | |
| Mentor shares teaching materials with mentee. | |
| Mentor and mentee arrange to meet periodically for informal chats. | |
| Mentor and mentee arrange to meet formally to discuss teaching, preparation and progress in adapting to the new job. | |
| Mentor sets mentee tasks, such as *self-observation and reflection* or *getting feedback from learners*, and requests feedback on these tasks. | |
| Mentor encourages mentee to e-mail reflections on their teaching and to raise any concerns they have. | |

### Step Five

Direct the mentee to some of the activities in *The Developing Teacher*, particularly those on self-observation and reflection, and getting feedback from students. The activity *Six ways of talking* from circle five is useful for both of you, as it deals with effective communication.

### Step Six

Start your mentoring. Plan tasks, meetings and deadlines for the month, using your diaries. Good luck!

### Step Seven

At the end of the month, evaluate the scheme with your mentee (and director of studies, perhaps). You can both consider these questions:

- Did you achieve your objectives?
- What else did you get out of the programme?
- Which elements of the programme were most effective?
- How could the programme have been improved?

You may decide to continue mentoring. If so, repeat Steps Four to Seven.

# You and your school

## The fourth circle

In circle three, we looked at development activities which involve informal collaboration with colleagues in the classroom and the staffroom. We now take one step further, incorporating activities which involve the school management and fellow teachers in an institutional setting.

Developmental activities with your school work on all four areas in the RISE model. Imposition and Recognition are likely to feature more than in previous circles. Schools can impose materials, training schemes, observation, quality control, and so on, and your response to these challenges will form an important part of your development. You can gain recognition if you respond effectively, as well as suggesting some initiatives of your own.

Opposite is a checklist of possible development actions and opportunities involving you in the wider context of your school. Which are of particular interest to you? Which have you already done? Which have you not thought of doing? Which might you like to concentrate on? Read the list and give yourself a score for each item.

There are two important features of institutional development: the concept of 'interdependence' and the idea of growth for both you and your school.

### Moving towards interdependence

Stephen Covey describes three stages of personal development. 'Dependence' (I need others to do things for me), 'independence' (I can do things for myself) and 'interdependence' (I realise I can achieve even more through working with others).

If we apply this model to teaching, we think of the newly-qualified teacher, *dependent* on guidance from senior teachers, trainers and coursebooks; the experienced teacher, *independent*, able to function effectively without outside help; and the *interdependent* teacher, ready to help other teachers and to engage with their colleagues, their school and their profession.

The fourth circle is about interdependent development, arguably the most challenging and the most satisfying. Now we have fitted our own oxygen mask, we turn our attention to helping others fit theirs and to working together to address challenges that we have in common.

### Growing with your school

For you and your school to grow together effectively, you will need to engage with other teachers and management in formal contexts, such as staff meetings and job appraisals, as well as the more informal interactions we have looked at.

**Personal checklist**

There are developmental actions you can take in the context of your school, its staff and administration. Read down the list.

- Give yourself a score from 0-5 for each item, according to how often you do it (0 = 'never done this', 5 = 'done this a lot').
- Then complete the right-hand column, adding a tick (✔) where appropriate, if you would like to try something, or do more of it

| Things I have done (or not done) … | Score (0-5) | (✔) |
|---|---|---|
| Participated in staff meetings | | |
| Proposed academic innovation | | |
| Proposed administrative innovation | | |
| Participated in the marketing of the school | | |
| Improved the appearance of the staffroom | | |
| Organised a social event | | |
| Worked on a project with colleagues/management | | |
| Participated in teacher workshops | | |
| Thought about how I communicate with colleagues | | |
| Approached my boss about my development | | |
| Worked on my communication skills | | |

**Comment**

Looking at this list should help identify areas of particular interest for you (or areas that you hadn't perhaps thought of) and will help you decide which of the activities you would most like to do.

A school, like any community or organisation, will have its traditions, politics and personalities, which will require careful handling. For this reason, activity will draw on ideas from outside ELT – from the fields of leadership, management and communication, encouraging you to think about and develop the skills which will help you become a more effective team member and team leader. You will address issues which affect everyone in the school and will work together with colleagues and management. You won't be able to do these activities on your own!

This fourth circle is divided into two sections, with activities which approach development on multiple fronts, from general communication and organisational skills to more specific developmental actions.

### Approaching change

The terms leadership and management refer to skills which

all of us use at work and other spheres of our lives, to address challenges and bring about change. They are not simply terms which describe what bosses do! Every one of us is called upon to lead and to manage at various times in our day-to-day lives.

*Leading and managing* explores how we can promote effective development. In classrooms, teachers naturally find themselves using leadership and management skills in helping their students to learn. Outside class, we can find it challenging to transfer these skills to promote our own professional growth and the growth of the organisation where we work.

*Circles of influence*, adapted from Stephen Covey, addresses the issue of what we can and can't change, individually and together. We need to be both realistic about the limitations of our influence, and optimistic about our ability to grow our influence. The more we understand this, the more effectively we can choose our activities and interventions.

*A good school* looks at what makes just that: a good school. Opinions will vary, of course! Whether you feel very positive about the place you work or whether you have mixed feelings, considering how you can improve your working environment is a very worthwhile activity which will help you set an agenda for development with your colleagues.

If the first activities in this circle are about setting a course, defining *what* we can and want to achieve, we now address the problem of carrying projects through, whether they be little, as in *Coffee stains*, or large, as in *SMARTER planning*. This is about *how* we achieve our developmental aims: how, for example, we approach our frequent and often inefficient teachers' meetings. How can we help to incorporate improvements and even innovation?

Teachers do not always speak positively of meetings at school. The six main complaints seem to be:

- Lack of clear aims
- Boring objectives, such as going over administration
- Meetings dominated by one or two people
- Time wasted in idle chat
- Too many people in the meeting, lack of pair- or groupwork to increase participation
- Poor timing

Most of these complaints can be rectified by applying the same criteria to meetings as we do to learning activities in the classroom – by thinking about how to get the most out of them, and also considering alternative ways to achieve our objectives.

## Approaching colleagues

Working with people we don't know, people we possibly don't like, and people who have authority over us in an organisation, isn't easy. We need to think about and improve on our communication skills. This may sound odd. Aren't teachers by definition good at communicating with people? There are three points to consider:

- Teachers are not always able to transfer classroom skills to the world outside. For example, some teachers are very good at listening to students, but very bad at listening to colleagues.
- The communication skills required for effective interaction with colleagues, parents and managers are possibly different to those required for dealing with students and, as they are used less frequently, may require more practice.
- Communication outside the classroom is often taken for granted. Teachers don't tend to plan and reflect on staffroom conversations, or what they say and do in meetings, in the same way as they might plan what they will say in a lesson.

John Heron's 'Six Categories of Intervention', or ways of conducting conversations, is aimed at professionals in jobs which require giving feedback, support and guidance to individual clients, and was adapted for the context of language teaching by Jim Scrivener. *Six ways of talking* helps you to think about the way you speak to and listen to other people and to evaluate the effects of *what you say*, as well as *what you do*.

*Place, Manner, Time* also invites you to reflect on how effective our conversations are from the point of view of *where* they take place, *how* (with what tone of formality) and *when*.

Colleagues, of course, also include managers and bosses. We often feel threatened by our employer or director of studies, and consequently spend our time fearing, or even avoiding, appraisal and feedback. In many schools, formal appraisal and the dreaded evaluative observation by a director of studies or senior teacher are common practice. In others, they are not. Whichever kind of place you work in, or even if you work as a freelance teacher, it is a good idea to turn these situations around, to put your head in 'the lion's mouth'. And who better to offer an opinion and to agree to institutional cooperation and innovation than your boss? Why not take a pro-active approach in your relationship, and get it straight from 'the horse's mouth'?

In the fourth circle, as we have seen, you carry your development forward hand in hand with your school, your teaching colleagues, administration staff and your boss(es). You discuss, plan and evaluate. You develop, and your colleagues and your school do, too.

In the fifth and final circle, you will take a final step beyond the school boundaries, involving yourself in developmental activities which will impact on ELT as your profession.

# Leading and managing
## Two approaches to challenges

### Rationale
In the classroom, teachers are both leaders and managers. It is useful to explore this distinction and apply it to solving problems outside the classroom, too. Being aware of two approaches to problem solving will help you to take effective steps and understand the responses you get from others.

### Activity
You reflect on the differences between *leading* and *managing*, and apply this distinction to some typical challenges at work.

### Step One
Working with a colleague, think of ways in which teachers are 'leaders' and 'managers' for their students. Look together at the quote from Stephen Covey below and then discuss your own ideas.

> *Management is a bottom-line focus: How can I best accomplish certain things? Leadership deals with the top line: What are the things I want to accomplish? In the words of Peter Drucker and Warren Bennis 'management is doing things right; leadership is doing the right things'.*

### Step Two
Look at the pairs of words opposite and decide which refers to *leading* (L) and to *managing* (M). The first two have been done for you. There is a key at the bottom of the page.

### Step Three
Referring back to the pairs of words, tell your partner about an occasion when you have been a *manager* for your students and one where you have been a *leader*.

### Step Four
Now look at the scenarios below. Choose two or three which are of particular interest to you. For each one, think of and discuss a *leader* response and a *manager* response to the challenge, and decide the pros and cons of each response. An example has been done for you.

- The coursebook you are using is not very relevant to your students.
- You think you are overworked/deserve a pay rise.
- A parent has complained about her child's progress.
- The classroom is always in a mess from the previous class when you arrive.
- You find staff meetings boring and not useful.

### Step Five
Look back at your responses in Step Four. Do you favour the leader or manager responses in general? What about your colleague? You will probably agree that both responses have merits, sometimes one more than the other, depending on the situation. Sometimes a combination is best.

### Leading or managing?

| change | L | M | stability |
|---|---|---|---|
| subordinates | M | L | followers |
| vision | | | objectives |
| sets direction | | | plans detail |
| formal authority | | | personal charisma |
| re-active | | | pro-active |
| passion | | | control |
| breaks rules | | | makes rules |
| takes blame | | | blames others |
| minimises risks | | | takes risks |
| new roads | | | existing roads |

### Leader or manager?

| Half of your students don't do the homework you set. | |
|---|---|
| **Leader response** | **Manager response** |
| *Set more interesting homework.* | *Introduce incentive for doing homework, or penalty for not doing it.* |
| **Pros:** *Students could be more motivated to do it.* **Cons:** *Might not necessarily relate to the syllabus requirements.* | **Pros:** *Could encourage more students to do homework.* **Cons:** *Might only work short-term.* |
| **You think you are overworked.** | |
| **Leader response** | **Manager response** |
| | |
| **Pros:** **Cons:** | **Pros:** **Cons:** |

### Step Six
Think of some scenarios that affect you directly, and discuss those. Try to consider both *leading* and *managing* when taking on developmental activity: this requires close collaboration with colleagues and bosses and will work better if you have an awareness of the roles and responses of leadership and management in effecting change.

### Key: Leading or managing?
**Leading:** change / followers / vision / sets direction / personal charisma / pro-active / passion / sell / breaks rules / takes blame / takes risks / new roads

# Circles of influence

## Building your influence in your school

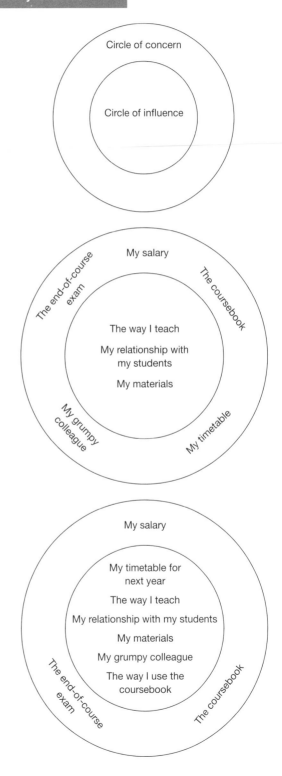

### Rationale

It is important for us to focus our limited time and energy on acting where we can make a difference, rather than worrying about things we can't influence. This activity, adapted from Stephen Covey, helps you to think about growing your *circle of influence* and reducing your *circle of concern* in the context of your workplace.

### Activity

You reflect on your working life and decide on the areas you can influence and those you can't, by using circle diagrams. You can work on your own, but this works better if you compare with a colleague or colleagues and brainstorm ideas together.

### Step One

Look at how we can represent things that worry us in two circles, as in the top diagram. The circle in the centre is the **circle of influence** and contains elements in your life, in this case your working life, which worry you but you feel you have influence or control over. The outer circle is the **circle of concern**. It contains elements which worry you but which you feel you *cannot* influence in any way.

### Step Two

Draw two circles and write in some elements from your life. See opposite for a sample diagram.

### Step Three

Now reconsider your circles. Think about how you could expand the inner circle by moving some elements from the outer circle. To do this, you will have to think about *ways* you can influence those elements.

### Step Four

Work with a partner. Discuss and help each other with suggestions.

### Step Five

Draw two new circles, with the middle one expanded. The third diagram is an example of how the circles might be changed. Here, the teacher has decided that while the choice of coursebook is outside their influence, the way they use it isn't. They have also moved *My timetable* to the circle of influence, perhaps because they feel they can negotiate this with their school.

### Step Six

Working with a new partner, if possible, explain the changes you have made in your circles. Can either of you think of further changes? Use the insights you have gained from this activity about *influence* to make decisions concerning how to build your influence in your school.

# A good school

## What makes a good work environment?

### Rationale

What is important to you and your colleagues in terms of your working environment? This diagnostic activity will help you to decide, and to think about what you want to change about it.

### Activity

You come to a consensus with some colleagues in a pyramid discussion on what makes your school a good place to work, and consider making improvements.

### Step One

Working on your own first of all, look at the list opposite of possible features of a good school. Add three more of your own if you wish. Your colleagues do likewise.

### Step Two

Working with a partner (you are A and B), tell each other what you have added to the list. Discuss and reach a consensus on the 'top six' most important features of a good school. Both of you make a note of your agreed top six on a piece of paper.

### Step Three

Now all the As group together and all the Bs group together and you repeat the exercise. You each read your lists to the other members of the group and reach a consensus within the group. Each group puts its list on the board.

### Step Four

Everyone now discusses the two lists and reaches a consensus on one single list.

### Step Five

Make a poster with this list, and put it up in the staffroom.

### Step Six

You may want to do this final step as a separate activity, depending on the time you have available. Work first with a single partner.

- Choose one of the six areas you would like to improve in the school.
- Brainstorm ideas on how to improve it.
- Decide on one thing you propose to do, making notes using the Pro-forma opposite. An example has been made for you.
- Explain your idea to another pair. If they approve, carry out your proposals.

Referring to the activity *Circles of influence* can help to ensure that your proposals are realistic.

---

**Features of a good school**

- Trust
- Mutual respect
- Clear communication
- Change
- Stability
- Sense of ownership or belonging
- Participation
- Feedback on how you are doing
- Praise
- Resources
- Consultation
- Clear rules
- Fun
- Attractive environment
- 
- 
- 

---

**Proposals for a better school**

| Proposal | What to do? | When? |
|----------|-------------|-------|
| Improving the appearance of classrooms by having work displayed on the walls. | Send a circular e-mail to other teachers and DOS to brainstorm ideas for activities which will generate wall displays. Choose one and do it. | Aim to have walls decorated by the end of November. |

# Coffee stains

## Dealing with small irritations at work

### Rationale

'Coffee stains' is a term that can describe small irritations at work, such as the room being stuffy, a poor quality CD player, mess from the previous class, a deficient photocopier or a grumpy colleague. They are not hugely important, but without cleaning up they can accumulate, and demoralise us.

### Activity

You think about the 'coffee stains' in your work and how to clean them up quickly and efficiently.

---

### Step One

Make yourself a cup of real coffee or get one from the machine. Try not to spill any!

### Step Two

Sit down and make a list of three coffee stains in your work. They can be in class, in the staffroom, or with specific people.

### Step Three

Write them in the left-hand column of the Pro-forma below.

**Coffee stains**

| What irritates me | What I can do about it | When and how I can do it |
|---|---|---|
| 1 | | |
| 2 | | |
| 3 | | |

### Step Four

Now choose one of the stains to clean up first. Decide *how* you can do it, and *when*, and write it in the Pro-forma. Make sure you commit to cleaning up the coffee stain by putting it in your diary (or acting immediately). An example is given for you.

**Cleaning stains**

| What irritates me | What I can do about it | When and how I can do it |
|---|---|---|
| The room I teach in at 5pm is always in a terrible mess when I get there. | Talk to the teacher of the previous class. Suggest she allows three minutes at the end of class for tidying up. I'll do the same. Circulate an e-mail to all the teachers, suggesting this as policy? | I see her Tuesday and Thursday mornings in the staffroom. I'll talk to her this Thursday. This is a better time than at the changeover, when we are both in a rush. |

# SMARTER planning

## Making sure you get the job done

### Rationale

We often generate great ideas for our personal development or making improvements at work, but find it difficult to make them happen. This activity gives you a framework to make it easier to transform good intentions into results.

### Activity

You plan a project with colleagues, using the SMARTER framework.

---

### Step One

Look at the acronym SMARTER below, which gives us a useful tool for elaborating on and refining objectives.

### Step Two

Working with a colleague or colleagues, agree on an innovation or improvement you would like to make to your school, your course or your teaching. In the example, you would like the students in the school to read more English outside class.

### Step Three

Refine your project by discussing your SMARTER objectives, building in the timeframe and feedback mechanism.

### Step Four

Try some more SMARTER planning, perhaps in new groups, with one or more projects, such as using DVD/YouTube clips more, sharing materials, getting feedback, helping teachers get to know each other, and so on.

**SMARTER objectives**

| | |
|---|---|
| **S**pecific | *For all the students to read one book by the end of November.* |
| **M**easurable | *Each teacher reports on how many of their students have read a book.* |
| **A**greed | *Yes, by teachers. Need to get the students to agree, too.* |
| **R**ealistic | *Need to use graded readers. Do we have enough graded readers? Teachers will have to encourage, monitor and do support work on reading skills. Ambitious? Do a pilot project with just a few classes?* |
| **T**imebound | *November 30th deadline.* |
| **E**thical/ Exciting | *Worthwhile to get the students reading more. It will help their language acquisition.* |
| **R**ecorded | *Send e-mail to the teachers concerned, outlining the project. Teachers to report on the results by Nov 30th.* |

# Meetings, meetings

## How to make the most of our meetings

### Rationale

It is common practice in many schools to call frequent face-to-face meetings, although they are not always positive experiences for participants. If that is the case in your place of work, you can help to improve the situation.

### Activity

You and some colleagues think about how effective the meetings in your school are, and consider alternatives.

### Step One

Working with two colleagues, think about recent meetings you have attended or organised. Do this from memory, or use the published agendas if they exist. Organise what you think happened into four categories, using the Pro-forma below. There is an example in each column.

| Meetings, meetings | | | |
|---|---|---|---|
| Social achievements | Administrative achievements | Creative achievements | Other things that happened |
| Got to know two new teachers. | Was told about the new policy on use of the photocopier. | Discussed ideas for using the internet more effectively to help students learn. | Listened to a colleague complaining about two students in their class. |

### Step Two

Choose three items from your Pro-forma and, for each one, discuss with your colleagues the following:
- Could it have been achieved more effectively in the meeting?
- Could it have been achieved more effectively without having a meeting. If so, how?
- Was it useful for everyone in the meeting?

### Step Three

Now look at the fourth column. Could the items there be eliminated or converted into achievements? Is this column too long, or too full?

### Step Four

If you are someone who initiates meetings, use the reflections from this activity to help you plan more effective meetings in the future. If you are someone who attends meetings but doesn't initiate them, think about how you can use these reflections to influence those that do.

# Meetings, what meetings?

## How to hold meetings without meeting

### Rationale

Many schools call face-to-face meetings to discuss policy and take decisions. In many cases, alternative forms of communication can be more effective. This activity can be combined with the activity *Meetings, meetings*.

### Activity

To lead and moderate an e-mail or wiki discussion with colleagues.

### Step One

Look at the agenda for your next meeting at work.

### Step Two

Choose an item which involves discussion and decision making. For example: changes to the third level end-of-term exam, discipline problems, choosing a new coursebook, the end-of-term party.

### Step Three

Send a group e-mail* to the colleagues involved, putting the item you have chosen as the title of the e-mail.

In the text of the e-mail, do the following:
- Briefly summarise the issue.
- Invite colleagues to contribute to a discussion on the issue via e-mail. Remind them to always 'reply all', so that everyone has a chance to read what they say.
- Set a time limit for the discussion (eg one week).

### Step Four

Monitor the discussion through the week. If participation is low, encourage your colleagues with brief responses to messages received and invitations to others to respond.

### Step Five

At the end of the week, summarise the key points from the discussion and list the action points/policy decisions.

*If your school has a wiki, blog, or Moodle, you can use one of these tools instead of e-mails.

# Six ways of talking

## Improving communication with colleagues

### Rationale

Unfortunate conversations, as much as unfortunate events, can be a cause of stress and confusion at work. This activity (based on John Heron's Six Category Intervention Analysis) helps you to understand and reflect on how you communicate with other people at work and how you could do it better.

### Activity

With colleagues, you roleplay 'difficult' conversations at work and analyse the communication achieved.

### Step One

Look at the six categories of 'intervention', or types of talk, in the box opposite.

### Step Two

Think about a conversation you have had recently at work with a colleague or boss, or with a student. What types of intervention did you make? Make a few notes on what was said. Your colleagues do likewise.

### Step Three

Working with a partner, talk about your thoughts and what you noted down. Discuss whether you thought the conversations were effective. Could you have spoken differently?

### Step Four

Now work in groups of three (A, B and C). A and B will act out a roleplay for about five minutes. C should listen and note down the types of interventions they hear.

### Step Five

Choose one of the 'six-way' roleplays in the box and do it.

### Step Six

Afterwards, discuss what the observer noted down. What types of intervention did B use? What other interventions would have been possible?

### Step Seven

Change your ABC roles and do some more roleplays. Use the examples here or write your own, related to your own personal work situation.

**Types of talk**

| Intervention | Definition | Example |
|---|---|---|
| Supportive | Helping or being sympathetic | *It must be hard when the children behave like that.* |
| Catalytic | Provoking the person to think about change | *How do you think they might change their behaviour?* |
| Confronting | Referring directly to unpleasant truths | *Was your lesson boring?* |
| Cathartic | Helping the other person express their feelings | *How do you feel?* |
| Informative | Providing information | *I know a good website with ideas for motivating teenagers.* |
| Prescriptive | Giving advice | *You should talk to the director of studies.* |

**'Six-way' roleplays**

**A:** You are an intermediate student. You are very unhappy about your progress in English. You decide to talk to your teacher about the situation after class one day.

**B:** You are a teacher. One of your students asks to speak to you after class one day.

**A:** You are a teacher. You are having problems with low attendance in one of your classes. You decide to speak to your director of studies about it

**B:** You are a director of studies. A teacher comes to speak to you about a problem they are having.

**A:** You are a director of studies. Some students have complained about one of the teachers. They say there is too much grammar in the lesson and they don't speak enough. You decide to talk to the teacher in your office.

**B:** You are a teacher. The director of studies has asked to speak to you in their office.

**A:** You are a teacher. You are in the staffroom and stuck for ideas for a class you are teaching later today. You decide to ask a colleague for help.

**B:** You are in the staffroom. A colleague asks for some help with a class they are anxious about.

# Place, Manner, Time

## Planning conversations at work

### Rationale

Many conversations are less successful than they could be because they happen in the wrong place, at the wrong time or with the wrong degree of formality; or perhaps all three! Reflecting on the PMT factors will help you to understand and achieve better interactions with colleagues.

### Activity

You and your colleagues think about *where*, *how* and *when* conversations take place at work, and the effect this has on them.

---

### Step One

Look at the list of possibilities in the first table opposite.

### Step Two

Working alone, think about a conversation you have had recently at work with a colleague, boss or with a student. Define the PMT. Your colleagues do likewise.

### Step Three

Working with a partner, discuss whether you thought the conversations were effective. How would a different PMT have made a difference?

### Step Four

Now working with a different partner, look at the roleplay scenarios opposite. Discuss what you think would be the most appropriate PMT for these conversations, and why.

### Step Five

Choose one or more of the roleplays to act out with your partner, according to the PMT you have discussed in Step Four. You may want to have a third person who can observe the conversation.

### Step Six

Discuss how successful the interaction was. Did planning the PMT help?

## The PMT of talk

| Place | Manner | Time |
|---|---|---|
| Staffroom | Formal, peer-peer | By appointment |
| Private office | | On the run |
| Corridor | Formal, boss-subordinate | After class |
| Bar/pub/café | | Defined duration |
| Classroom | Formal, teacher-student | Undefined duration |
| Reception area | Informal, peer-peer | In the heat of the moment |
| Home | Informal, boss-subordinate | After a cooling-off period |
| By the photocopier | | |
| E-mail | Informal, teacher-student | |

## PMT roleplays

**A:** You are a teacher. You would like the school to sponsor you to do a teacher development course.

**B:** You are the school director. A teacher has asked to see you about training.

**A:** You are a teacher. You have been ill for a week, and would like to talk to the teacher who covered your classes while you were absent about what they did.

**B:** You are a teacher. You have been covering a colleague's classes for a week while they were ill.

**A:** You are the director of studies. A member of staff hasn't been keeping their registers up to date. You would like to talk to them about it.

**B:** You are a teacher. The director of studies asks to see you.

**A:** You are a student. You think there is too much grammar in the class. You want to spend more time on conversation. You decide to speak to your teacher.

**B:** You are a teacher. One of your students asks to see you.

# The lion's mouth

## Getting feedback from your boss

### Rationale

It is easy to feel threatened by the idea of observation and appraisal from an employer or director of studies. If you can put yourself in charge of the situation, put your head 'in the lion's mouth', you will feel stronger and more confident about your teaching (and your boss will be impressed!).

### Activity

You take the initiative and ask your boss to observe your teaching.

---

### Step One

Find an opportunity to talk to your boss, either by appointment or casually in the staffroom. Think about the best way to do this (you can refer to *Place, Manner, Time* on page 70).

### Step Two

Explain that you would like them to observe you teaching because you feel you would benefit from having some feedback from someone with their experience.

### Step Three

Suggest an aspect of your teaching you would like them to focus on in particular. (See the activity *Be my judge* in circle three for some ideas.)

### Step Four

Fix a time and place for the observation, and agree a way of doing feedback (a brief discussion after the lesson, or by e-mail if either of you are busy).

### Step Five

No turning back now! You go ahead with the observation and the feedback.

### Step Six

Now you have put your 'head in the lion's mouth' you might want to do the same next year – unless of course it was bitten off!

# The horse's mouth

## Taking on new roles and instigating new activities

### Rationale

Rather than waiting to be asked, you can take a pro-active approach to finding new challenges and raising your profile in your school. By involving your boss, you will get some ideas straight from the horse's mouth! You can then plan to engage in something that will benefit both you and the school.

### Activity

You discuss with your boss how to link your personal development to something beneficial for the school.

---

### Step One

Request a meeting with your boss. Explain that you would like to discuss ways you can help the school to develop.

### Step Two

In the meeting, explain that you would like to take on a new challenge, as part of your own development as a teacher. Discuss suggestions for projects which could benefit both the school and you. Be clear about how much time you have available and that you do not expect remuneration.

### Step Three

Agree on a project. It should be something like a partnership, which benefits you personally in your development and is useful to the school. Below are some ideas, but you will both obviously have others.

**Partnership activities**

Make an inventory of teaching materials.
Create or improve a feedback questionnaire for students.
Organise a workshop for teachers.
Organise a film night for students.
Suggest a new course for students, and do some research to find out if there is demand.
Start a blog or wiki for staff or students.
Create a DVD library for teachers, with teaching materials.
Improve an end-of-course exam.

### Step Four

Use SMARTER objectives to define the parameters of your chosen project (see page 67). Do this together with your boss or director of studies, or prepare a plan yourself and e-mail it to them for comments and suggestions.

### Step Five

Do it.

### Step Six

Report back via e-mail or meet again, to discuss the outcome. Was the project a success for the school and for you? Would you like to take on another project?

# You and your profession

## The fifth circle

The activities in circle four related to development in your school. We now move one final step outwards. The activities here involve engaging in some way with what we might call 'the profession', *your* profession.

We can use this term to describe the organisations and practices which link and regulate the language teaching profession. For example:

- Exam bodies providing teacher training and English language qualifications
- Teachers' associations, such as IATEFL
- Teacher support groups
- ELT publishers and websites

This is obviously the widest of the five circles we work in and involves varying degrees of difficulty and involvement. Publishing an article about motivating teenagers is a more ambitious project than trialling a new piece of material with your teenage learners. Writing for a wide audience or speaking at a conference are substantial challenges. In this circle, you will again work on R, I, S and E.

- Recognition – as your contribution is noted by fellow teachers
- Imposition – if you submit to the demands of a formal qualification
- Self-improvement – as always!
- Enjoyment – in this case, from new challenges, working with different people and perhaps travel

Opposite is a checklist of possible professional development actions and opportunities. Read the list and give yourself a score for each item. Which of the things are of particular interest to you? Which have you already done? Which have you not thought of doing? Which might you like to try?

The developmental focus in this circle is divided into three sections, covering the areas of options for qualifications; writing for publication, speaking at conferences, and linking up with other ELT professionals; planning and organising your priorities, thinking about *what* you want to achieve and *how to commit* to achieving it.

### A qualified teacher

You may already hold a battery of qualifications, you may not have any. The diversity of the ELT profession and the range of face-to-face and online options for training can make choosing a course or professional qualification difficult. The two activities in this section focus on helping you to decide the best option for you to enhance your future development as a teacher.

---

### Personal checklist

There are things you can do in your professional capacity to develop yourself and your teaching. Read down the list.

- Give yourself a score from 0-5 for each item, according to how often you do it (0 = 'never done this', 5 = 'done this a lot').
- Then complete the right-hand column, adding a tick (✔) where appropriate, if you would like to try something, or do more of it

| Things I have done (or not done) ... | Score (0-5) | (✔) |
|---|---|---|
| Attended a conference | | |
| Been a member of an online teachers' group | | |
| Lead a workshop or talk at a conference | | |
| Written material for a website or in print | | |
| Written an article for a website or in print | | |
| Written a book | | |
| Created my own teaching-related website | | |
| Considered my career aims | | |
| Completed a course leading to a qualification such as a Diploma or Masters | | |
| Completed a professional development course | | |
| Trialled material for a publisher | | |

**Comment**
Looking at this list should help identify areas of particular interest for you (or areas that you hadn't perhaps thought of) and will help you decide which of the activities you would most like to do.

---

### A professional teacher

These activities are designed to support those of you who want to take on the challenges of writing and public speaking in ELT – being 'a professional', beyond the confines of the classroom or even the school. It needn't be as big a step as you think! The step-by-step approach taken here will help you build on your teacher skills and transfer them to a more public arena.

**Writing** for publication can be an unfamiliar activity for most teachers. Writing itself, though, isn't; at least, not any more. It has become increasingly important in the 21st century to communicate in this way, with e-mails, blogs and forums being the medium of choice where once telephone calls, meetings and face-to-face debate would have prevailed. Because blogs and forums are often public, the line between published and unpublished writing has become less clearly drawn. We are all published writers in a sense. From the point of view of your professional development, the question is not *whether* you are read, but *how widely* you are read and with what degree of *interest*.

You can develop your writing (in terms of skills and confidence) by breaking down and unwrapping the task in hand, just as you do for your students. In the activities in previous circles you have written reflections, diary entries, e-mails, lesson plans, and so on. This circle takes writing one step further, as you learn to shape and direct what you write and how to write to meet the needs of a wider readership, whether trialling material for an ELT publisher and writing a report, writing an article, or writing a report on a conference you have attended.

**Speaking**, however, is the subject of the first activity in this section. The growth of written discourse doesn't mean that the good old-fashioned workshop is dead! Far from it. Teachers attend workshops in schools, universities and conferences around the globe. But with the increasing support of electronic media and use of written media to transmit ideas, participants will be looking for unique benefits when attending workshops or talks. Speeches and handouts can be easily downloaded. Charisma, spontaneous interaction, participation and a sense of community, less so.

The activity *BEN HUR* provides steps and tools for planning a workshop which will be as exciting as a chariot race!

### A developing teacher

Teacher learning, like language learning, can be divided into the four skills: reading, writing, listening and speaking. Or if you prefer, productive and receptive skills. It is useful to think about which you are most comfortable with. A developing teacher might commit to a small developmental task each month for four months, for example: one involving each of the four skills. You block time in your diary to do it and will probably break the task down into several mini-sessions.

The examples of developmental activities opposite are divided into the four skills. Choose one skill to start with.

When the four months have passed and you have done four developmental activities, you can reflect by considering these questions:

- Which did I get the most from?
- Which did I enjoy the most/least?
- Do I have a preferred skill?

If you do have a preferred skill, then make the most of it!

In *Back to the future*, you think about your aims. It is good to reflect in the longer term and visualise what you think you will have achieved by the time you say goodbye to the profession. This activity reveals what it is you *want* to achieve.

But you also have to think about what you want to do in

| Skillful resolutions | | | |
|---|---|---|---|
| **Reading** | **Writing** | **Listening** | **Speaking** |
| Books for teachers | Write an article for a website or ELT magazine or newsletter. | Watch a DVD of some teaching. | Give a workshop at your school or another school. |
| An academic text | Write a report on an ELT event for your school or a local newspaper. | Go to a workshop. | Give a workshop/ talk at a conference. |
| An ELT magazine or newsletter | Write a letter to the editor of a magazine. | Find a podcast relating to ELT and subscribe. | Go to a conference or event and make contact with three teachers from other schools. |
| An ELT website | Write an e-mail to an author/ publisher. | Meet a colleague for one hour to discuss an issue that interests you both. | |

the more immediate future – to commit, to get involved, to decide what it is you want *to be* and where you want *to go*. In *Decisions, decisions!* you plan for the achievement of your longer-term aims, with considerations of three longer projects than the short activities that have been presented with so far in *The Developing Teacher*, and you take a vital step to committing further to your profession.

An important feature of this book has been to encourage you to reflect on your developmental aims and how you want to achieve them. Deciding *what* you want to happen and *why*, then *how* and *when* to make it happen, are the 'meta' activities which shape and direct the rest.

We have attempted to address the two 'elephant questions' of teacher development:

- Why should I?
- How can I?

We have raised the questions. Only you can provide the answers.

# RISE up

## Choosing a teaching qualification

### Rationale

The range of qualifications on offer to English teachers can make it difficult to know which to choose. The diversity of the profession makes it important to choose the right qualification for your situation and your future career.

### Activity

To choose a qualification that will upgrade your ongoing development, open up opportunities and raise your professional status.

### Step One

Some questions, the answers to which can help you choose a course, can once again be summarised in our acronym RISE. Read the questions in the checklist opposite.

### Step Two

Do some research. You may already have a qualification in mind but it is a good idea to look around, as this will help you understand your choice or even lead to a different choice. Find two or three options. Remember you can consider qualifications which are not directly related to TEFL, such as a language qualification or a business qualification.

- Look on the internet and in ELT magazines for information.
- Ask colleagues/your boss for recommendations.
- Join discussion forums and ask for further information and recommendations.
- Look at the qualifications of people in positions you aspire to.

### Step Three

Evaluate the options you have found, using the 'RISE up' checklist.

### Step Four

Fill in the options table opposite with notes in each category and a rating out of 5 for each.

### Step Five

Choose the qualification you want, and apply!

---

### RISE up checklist

**R**ecognition
Who recognises this qualification and why? Will it open up new job opportunities for me? Will it give me higher status? Can I earn more if I have this qualification?

**I**mposition
Is the qualification required for me to maintain my present job? Has it been imposed by my employer? Am I imposing it on myself as something I feel obliged to undertake to be 'marketable'?

**S**elf-improvement
Will the preparation/course for the qualification improve my job satisfaction and my sense of self-worth? Will it make me a better teacher?

**E**njoyment
Will the preparation/course be enjoyable?

---

### RISE up options

|  | Option 1 | Option 2 | Option 3 |
|---|---|---|---|
| **R** | Rating: | Rating: | Rating: |
| **I** | Rating: | Rating: | Rating: |
| **S** | Rating: | Rating: | Rating: |
| **E** | Rating: | Rating: | Rating: |
| Cost: |  |  |  |
| Time: |  |  |  |
| Other factors: |  |  |  |

# Course, what course?

## Choosing a short professional development course

### Rationale

There are a lot of professional development courses on offer for teachers. This activity is designed to help you decide how to choose the most effective one for you.

### Activity

To review and evaluate options for a professional development course and choose one.

### Step One

Opposite is a checklist of six possible *outcomes* from a professional development course. Score each one from 0–5, according to how important it is for you. Add up to two further possible outcomes in the spaces below.

### Step Two

Now consider the checklist of nine course models and give each a mark out of 5, according to how *appealing* it is to you.

### Step Three

Finally, consider your own situation very carefully and very honestly:

- Why do you *want* to do a course?
- Do you *need* a qualification?
- Can you take time off?
- Can you afford it?

### Step Four

Now you should have a clearer idea of what you are looking for. Use the categories where you scored highly in Steps One and Two, and make your own checklist when evaluating courses on offer.

### Step Five

Plan some time and set yourself a time limit. Do some research:

- Look at websites and ELT magazines for information.
- Ask colleagues or your boss for recommendations.
- Find forums on the internet where courses are discussed for further information and recommendations.

### Step Six

If you find a course which meets your requirements (and your budget!), do it.

| Course outcomes | Score |
|---|---|
| I learn something which will help me in my current job. | |
| I learn something that interests me. | |
| I acquire marketable skills or expertise, eg how to teach online. | |
| The course is challenging so I will benefit from meeting the challenge. | |
| I make useful contacts on the course. | |
| The course leads to promotion/new job possibilities. | |
| | |
| | |

| Course appeal | Score |
|---|---|
| Online learning, with frequent contact with tutors and fellow students | |
| Online learning, with little or no contact with others | |
| Face-to-face learning, part-time | |
| Face-to-face learning, full-time intensive | |
| Course in my home country | |
| Course abroad | |
| Blended learning (a combination of online and face-to-face) | |
| Driven by expert input | |
| Driven by student input/collaboration | |

# BEN HUR

## Planning how to lead an effective workshop

### Rationale

As well as obliging you to articulate all your ideas coherently, leading a workshop helps you develop your self-esteem as a teacher. You can develop your own communication skills and sense of community with other teachers. Don't feel daunted: a workshop is not a lecture, it is more like a staffroom chat with some very careful organization.

### Activity

To plan a successful workshop with the help of a checklist.

---

### Step One
#### Brainstorming

- Think about what your own areas of interest or expertise are, or what unique experiences you have, which might be shared with colleagues.
- Think about your audience and what will be useful and enjoyable for them (the BEN HUR checklist opposite will help). If you are doing a workshop in your school, check with the teachers who will be attending about their needs and interests.
- Think about good workshops you have attended and what made them good.

### Step Two
#### Planning

- There is no single, correct way to organise a workshop. Plan in the same way as you do a language class, thinking about the participants and their needs, and your aims and activities.
- Think about what you want to say, your input (an anecdote, a schema, a list of tips).
- Think about what you will be getting participants to do in the workshop, your activities and what feedback you will get from them.
- Think about what materials you will need for all the above, and the timings.
- Plan the activities phase to last at least double the time of the input phase.

### Step Three
#### Checking

- Use the BEN HUR checklist to evaluate your plan.
- Check your plan with a colleague and make some changes following any suggestions.

### Step Four

Remember: the maxim 'teach the students, not the plan' applies to workshops, too! Be prepared to adapt your plan and respond to the participants.

Relax: you are now ready to lead a very successful workshop.

---

## BEN HUR

**B**uilding on the participants' experience
Participants have a chance to draw on their own experience and knowledge (of teaching or learning) and can feel they are building on these. Evolution is better than revolution.

**E**njoyment
This could derive from performance-related factors, such as personal charisma, humour, and clarity of visuals; or participatory factors, such as interaction with participants and working together on a task; plus a pleasant environment, with elements such as sunshine, comfort, music and refreshments. Or a combination of any of these.

**N**ovelty
Participants should feel that there is something new for them. This could be an approach, an activity, a new idea, a new angle on an old idea, etc.

**H**ard work
In input phases, challenge can come from listening and following new or complex ideas. In hands-on phases, challenge can come from the tasks the participants do, or the reflection and articulation required of them.

**U**nderstanding
Participants feel they have understood key messages and ideas and how they might be put into practice. In the case of ideas for specific activities, they understand exactly how they work.

**R**elevance
Participants need to see how the content of the workshop can be applied in their own teaching.

# Conference reporter

## Attending a conference and reporting back

### Rationale

Reporting on a conference you have been to, verbally or in writing, helps you to focus on what you have learnt. It may encourage your school to sponsor you: if they feel they are getting something in return!

### Activity

To go to a conference and report back to your colleagues (either in writing or as a workshop).

---

### Step One

Find a conference you would like to attend.

### Step Two

Before the conference, prepare a proposal for your director of studies.

- Outline the benefits of your going to the conference for *you* and for the *school*.
- Propose to report back on the conference in some way to staff via a workshop, a meeting, an e-mail, a conference file, etc.
- List the costs (conference fees, accommodation, travel, etc).
- Offer to pay some or all of the costs yourself.

### Step Three

At the conference, take notes, make contacts, collect free materials.

### Step Four

After the conference, prepare your report (written or verbal) or a workshop. Here are some ideas to help you:

- Don't feel you need to narrate the whole experience or relate every session you attended.
- If you choose to replicate one of the workshops you attended, acknowledge the author and their materials.
- For a report, or to organise your workshop, you could use a structure like this:

| Conference comments |
| --- |
| Best workshop I attended, and why: |
| Best published material I found, and why: |
| Most interesting contact I made, and why: |
| Most relevant to our school was … |

### Step Five

Circulate an e-mail of your report, with handouts and links, to all the staff. Invite your colleagues to comment and ask questions.

# Join the CoPs

## Participating in a community of practice

### Rationale

A community of practice (CoP) is a group of teachers formed online or face-to-face who share a common interest in some aspect of teaching, and come together to learn *with* and *from* each other. There are many benefits of joining one.

- You learn about teaching.
- You learn about how to work with other people.
- You make useful contacts.
- You derive satisfaction from making your own contribution.

### Activity

To research some communities of practice you could join, and join one.

---

### Step One

Before you look for a group to join, consider these three questions and make some notes:

| Communities of practice |
| --- |
| What do I want to get out of being in a group? |
| What am I prepared to put in? |
| How much time am I prepared to dedicate? |

### Step Two

Look on the internet for information about national and international teacher groups. Here are two sites to get you started:

- www.iatefl.org
- www.britishcouncil.org/eltecs

### Step Three

Do some more research and find information about local teacher groups. (If you can't find a local group, consider starting one yourself if you think there is interest.)

### Step Four

Choose one of the groups you found in Steps Two and Three, and join it.

### Step Five

Convince a colleague or fellow teacher to join the group.

# Salami writer

## Planning to write for ELT

### Rationale

Writing is an essential part of engaging with the teaching profession. You might feel daunted by the prospect of writing for an audience. Take a slice-by-slice approach to developing as a writer and you will gradually build your skill and confidence.

### Activity

To help you start writing, or move you forward if you have already started, perhaps with a book review.

### Step One

Look at the kinds of TEFL writing listed below. If you have already published, tick (✔) the ones you have done and had published. Put an asterisk (*) by the ones you want to do, or do more of.

| Writing for ELT | Done? |
| --- | --- |
| An essay or assignment for a professional qualification | |
| A contribution to an ELT forum or blog | |
| A letter to the editor of a magazine or newsletter | |
| A contribution to a newsletter | |
| A review of a conference | |
| Teaching material | |
| A book review | |
| An article | |
| A book | |

### Step Two

Look at where you have put the *s. Think about your (next) choice of writing project. Bear in mind these points:
- Some things are more difficult than others. It is easier to be published on a website than in print, for example.
- You can choose a project which repeats something you have done already or you can incorporate more challenge. Both have pros and cons. Think about them.
- You can write based on what interests *you* or what you have been told would be of interest to *readers* by the editor or website co-ordinator. Both have pros and cons. Think about them.
- Remember: you can do it!

### Step Three

Choose your writing project. Set yourself a deadline and block time in your diary to get the work done.
- Allow time for the following: reading; researching; writing; getting feedback; rewriting.
- Work backwards from your deadline, if you have one.

### Step Four

Write your piece. Get a colleague to check it. Revise it.

### Step Five

Send it.

# A book review

## The constructive critic

### Rationale

A review involves reacting to something *someone else* has written, and may be a good place to start. You can write a book review for colleagues in a teachers' group or staffroom, as part of a training course, or for publication in a teachers' journal. It can be of a coursebook, of a supplementary activities book or methodology book.

### Step One

Read some reviews of books: most journals have a section for book reviews. Notice how they are structured. Make notes of features of the reviews that you like.

### Step Two

Make notes, as in the list below, for the book you intend to review.
- Title/Author/Publisher
- What type of book is it and what does it contain?
- Who is it aimed at?
- In what way is it different to other books in the field?
- An example of a unit/activity/chapter
- Something you particularly like about the book
- A reservation you have about the book
- Your final evaluation. Who would find the book useful and why?

### Step Three

Turn your notes into your text. If the review is for informal circulation only, you could even leave it in note form.

### Step Four

Review what you have written and get a colleague to read it. Remember that, as readers, we tend to be interested in 'good reviews'. You can pick out faults, but keep the tone positive.

### Step Five

Send it.

# Writing your voice

## Preparing an article for publication

### Rationale

An article is a *pro-active* and *personal* perspective and is more difficult than a book review, for example. To write an article that voices your opinions, you need: something to say; the commitment to doing the work; a friend or colleague to give you some feedback.

### Activity

To write an article for publication on the web or in a professional journal.

### Step One

Read several articles on the web or in professional journals and make notes on what you *like* and *dislike* about them. Use this as a checklist when you come to write your own article later.

| I liked ... | I disliked ... |
|---|---|
|  |  |

### Step Two

Look at the selected list of article topics opposite, adapted from the British Council site at the time of writing: www.teachingenglish.org.uk.

If you had to write an article on one of these titles, which would you choose and why? Can you think of others?

### Step Three

With colleagues (if you can) think about your own teaching and make a list of six 'areas of interest' (see the Pro-forma opposite) that particularly interest *you*. Brainstorming works best if you accept anything that you think of, at least initially, and avoid the temptation to dismiss ideas quickly.

These ideas could be: a strategy or technique you use, a teaching idea, a social or political aspect of teaching English that interests you, or a method you have adapted to your own teaching situation. In short, if it interests you, it will probably interest other teachers.

### Step Four

Choose one of your six options from Step Three. Use your colleagues to help you.

### Step Five

Make some notes for your article using the final Pro-forma opposite to help you.

### Step Six

Turn your notes from Step Five into a draft version of the article.

## Topics of interest

- Creative writing
- Learning vocabulary
- Using articles in the news
- Listening for teenagers
- E-learning
- Arts and crafts with YL
- Using authentic materials
- Storytelling
- Portfolios
- Pronunciation through songs
- Large classes
- NLP
- Socio-cultural awareness
- Teaching one to one

## Areas of interest

| 1 |  |
|---|---|
| 2 |  |
| 3 |  |
| 4 |  |
| 5 |  |
| 6 |  |

## An article of interest

| Who will read it? |  |
|---|---|
| How long will it be? |  |
| Will it include visuals? (A diagram, table, illustration?) |  |
| In what way is it original? (Originality can be in the organisation or grouping of ideas, a new angle on an old theme, an adaptation of an idea from a different field ...) |  |
| Brief summary of what your article will contain (These could be sub-headings.) |  |

### Step Seven

Get someone to check it and give you feedback. Rewrite it!

### Step Eight

Send the article to an ELT website or magazine. Bear in mind that it is usually easier to be published on the former. Don't be discouraged if you aren't accepted the first time. Learn from the experience, and try again.

# Trial without error

## Trying out material for a publisher

### Rationale

Volunteering to trial material can contribute to your personal development by making you reflect on how material works. Your students may well also appreciate a sense of involvement in the process. You will be acknowledged in the final publication and will establish contact with the ELT publishing world.

### Activity

To try out some teaching material for a publisher.

### Step One

Choose some publishers of books you use or like. Find the relevant contact details, preferably a person 'editorial'.

### Step Two

Write an e-mail, offering to trial material. State briefly:

- who you are – your teaching context, and why yours would be a good context for this;
- why you would like to trial the material, and why you like that publisher's material, quoting examples.

### Step Three

Wait. If you get no reply or a 'not now but in the future sometime' response, wait three months and write again.

### Step Four

Trying out materials means trialling then writing a report. Give *evidence* that you used the material in class (who you used it with, how often, how long it took, etc). Publishers value the following, so try to fulfil their expectations:

---

#### Quality feedback

- **Informed feedback** – Refer where possible to other published material (methodology books, articles, workshops you attended or other coursebooks).
- **Constructive feedback** – Say if something *didn't* work and suggest what could make it better.
- **Balanced feedback** – Say what you *did* like, otherwise you seem like someone who is never satisfied.
- **Honest feedback** – If something is completely unusable, don't be afraid to say so.

---

### Step Five

Send your report to the publisher. Thank them for giving you the opportunity to participate. Let them know that you would be interested in repeating the experience (if indeed you are).

### Step Six

Should you think you can write material that's just as good, or better, than what you have been trialling, offer to send samples of your own work.

# Hidden treasure

## Preparing your own material for publication

### Rationale

Having shared your material with your students and perhaps your colleagues (see the activity *Sharing board* in circle three), why hide it from the profession at large? Take things one step further and get pubished! Publishers are often looking for teachers who can write supplementary materials for coursebooks and activities/lesson plans for websites. This is one of the few activities in *The Developing Teacher* which enhances your teaching and earns you money at the same time!

### Activity

To present a piece of material to be published.

### Step One

Prepare some material you have written and used in class. Make it look good.

### Step Two

Find a contact in the publishing world. You need someone in 'editorial'.

### Step Three

Make initial contact. Introduce yourself and offer your services as a writer. Explain your teaching context and your previous publications (if any, even on the web or a local magazine). Outline your interests (young learners, business, general, teenagers, etc).

### Step Four

All being well, you may be invited to submit a sample, according to specifications the publisher gives. Prepare your material carefully, perhaps using a Pro-forma like the one below, and send it.

| Planning to write | When? |
|---|---|
| Deadline: | |
| Preparation work needed: | |
| Doing the writing: | |
| Checked by someone: | |

### Step Five

If you are accepted, celebrate. You are going to be published!

If not, bear in mind that many would-be writers don't even bother going beyond Step Two above. Also, that very many samples are turned down. Don't be discouraged if you aren't accepted the first time. Learn from the experience, and try again. Think if there is any way you can adapt your material or its presentation for a more successful second try.

# Back to the future

## Visualising your career aims

### Rationale

Your career, like a language class, works better if you have some clear aims. Once your aims are clear, it will be easier to design your activities, the things that keep you busy.

### Activity

To think about the aims of your working life by placing yourself in the future, and looking back.

---

### Step One

Find a quiet place. Read and visualise the retirement party situation opposite.

### Step Two

Make some notes on what you and the other people at your party said in their speeches in the Pro-forma opposite.

### Step Three

What you wrote in Step Two are your career **aims**. Now consider your current **activities**. In what ways are they contributing to your aims? For example, think about your day at work today. In what way did it contribute to your aims?

### Step Four

Now ask yourself if there are any aims which are not being worked on. What could you change? Remember, you have five years!

### Step Five

Discuss your notes and thoughts with a colleague.

### Note

The activity is based on an idea from Stephen Covey's book *The Seven Habits of Highly Effective People*.

---

**Retirement party**

You are going to a retirement party. The time is five years from now.

You dress and make your way to the place where it is being held. It is a formal party, with speeches and groups of people sitting around tables. When you arrive you see the other guests waiting. You realise you don't know whose retirement party it is. You ask one of the guests the name of the person. They reply with *your* name. The party is for *your* retirement!

Who can you see at the party?

Where exactly is it?

What music is playing?

There are speeches at the party, one from you and others from colleagues and students, past and present.

What do *you* say?

What do *they* say?

Now leave the party.

---

**Retirement speeches**

| Me | |
|---|---|
| Colleagues | |
| Students | |

# Decisions, decisions!

## Committing to a longer-term project

### Rationale

Many long-term development projects never get off the ground because either the individual teachers or the school haven't paid enough attention to thinking the project through. They take a lot of work, so you are unlikely to finish them unless you are really committed. This activity helps you to consider the benefits and weigh them against the costs. It is best done with at least one other teacher.

### Activity

To consider the pros and cons of three long-term development projects and make a decision *whether* to do one, and *which* one.

### Step One

Read the descriptions of the three longer-term projects: a teacher diary, a teaching portfolio and a teacher development scheme in Part C of *The Developing Teacher*, on pages 84, 87 and 92.

### Step Two

Read the objections to each project made by teachers in the boxes opposite. Do you agree with them? If not, what are the counter arguments? Discuss with a colleague or colleagues, if possible.

### Step Three

Now work alone. Choose one of the three projects. Make a personal list of pros and cons for *you*.

### Step Four

Show your list to a colleague. Ask your colleague to play 'devil's advocate' and try to convince you not do it. They will argue, using your 'cons' list. You should argue in favour, using the 'pros' list. Exchange roles and do the same, each using the other list.

Alternatively, you can also do this the other way round: your colleague first plays 'angel's advocate' and tries to convince you to do the project.

### Step Five

Take a decision, *yes* or *no*, whether to do the project or not. If you decide yes, follow the *Step-by-step guide* for it in Part C. If you decide no, well, your work is done ... for now.

### Step Six

If you chose to commit to one of the three projects, you may want to return to this activity and commit to another at some point in the future. If you chose *not* commit to a project, you now have a clearer idea about what you want from teacher development and what you are prepared to put in to it. You are taking big steps, either way.

| I object to keeping a teacher diary ... | |
|---|---|
| I haven't got time for that ... I'd rather spend the time preparing the next lesson. | |
| I can't see how writing a diary is going to help my teaching. | |
| It's a bit self-indulgent, isn't it? Wouldn't it be better to discuss classes with my colleagues? | |
| I'm not very good at writing. I never know what to write. | |
| Diaries are for girls! | |

| I object to completing a teaching portfolio ... | |
|---|---|
| I haven't got time for that. It will take ages to put a portfolio together. I have better things to do with my time. | |
| Why should I make a portfolio? I know what I'm doing. I don't need to prove it. | |
| This is just appraisal by the back door, a way for the school to check up on us. | |
| My work is done in the classroom. A portfolio won't reflect that. | |
| Some people keep their photos neatly organised in albums, others have them stuffed in a drawer. It just depends on the kind of person you are. | |

| I object to teacher development schemes ... | |
|---|---|
| It's too much hassle to organise! | |
| I can organise my own development, I don't need a scheme. | |
| I don't have the authority to organise a scheme involving others. | |
| I'm not interested unless I'm paid to participate. | |
| If I try to organise one, my colleagues will resent me. | |

| I think ... | |
|---|---|
| Pros | Cons |
| | |

***The Developing Teacher*** aims to take your development one step further. So far, activities have been suggested which are, on the whole, short and designed to fit into and around your busy schedule. Development can also include long-term projects, and you will probably find there are points in your teaching career when you can dedicate yourself to taking these steps: you can do an MA, PhD or other practical or theoretical course, take a sabbatical year and do some research, do a job exchange or secondment for a year, and so on.

The three projects we are suggesting are not ongoing in that sense. They are, rather, 'elongated activities'. They have a defined ending and outcome, because that probably makes them easier and more motivating to do: they work from the premise that development is best conceived not as a continuous line, but a collection of moments. They encourage you to create and compile these moments, pause, reflect, celebrate, and then move on.

### Three longer-term projects

Here, then, we are looking at three projects which take a certain amount of time to complete: weeks or months, rather than days or hours.

- In the first project you keep a diary, where you reflect and comment on activities you have carried out.
- In the second and third projects you can incorporate a selection of these activities, combine them with other material from your professional practice, and collate and reflect on them.

Both the portfolio project and teacher development scheme encourage you to link up and group together elements, creating a whole which provides shape, form and direction to the smaller steps you take.

### Three circles of further development

These three projects can be visualised as concentric circles, moving from the individual and possibly private to the public and collaborative. Because they take some time, it is important to give them some careful consideration *before* making a commitment to seeing them through. The activity *Decisions, decisions!* at the end of circle five should have helped you to choose a particular project, by exploring the possible benefits and considering the drawbacks.

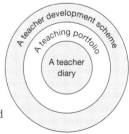

Some background information will first familiarise you with what each project entails and how it can help your development as a teacher. A detailed guide will then provide the support you need to help you get the most out of each one, as you step forward.

# A teacher diary 1

**A personal project**

A teacher diary, or teaching journal, is a written account of events that happen in the classroom and your reflections on them.

A diary can be private, for your eyes only, or public, ie shared with colleagues or published. It can be analysed by a researcher who is not the diarist (a 'diary study') or simply contain your unedited or 'raw' entries. It can focus on one group of students or a range of groups. It can focus on a single area of your teaching or can be open-ended. Diary entries can be written immediately after the class (hot entries) or at some later point (cool entries), and the diary can be kept for a short intensive period (say a week) or over an extensive period, such as a term. Here is a summary of the options:

- Private ···························· Public
- Language learning ················ Language teaching
- Raw entries only ·················· Diary study
- With a focus ······················· Without a focus
- About one class ················· About various classes
- Intensive ·························· Extensive

### What form can it take?

A diary can be handwritten, though it is more common to use a computer and keep an e-journal. This allows you to circulate your diary to others easily, should you choose to do so, and also allows you to add picture, video and sound files.

The form the diary takes will reflect your aims and what it contains. The handwritten diary is appropriate for private diaries and 'hot entries' when a computer may not be to hand. The e-journal is easy to share and publish.

### What can it contribute to your development?

We can refer again to our RISE acronym. Diaries are a good way to foster *self-improvement*. There is a difference between *writing* about teaching and *speaking* about teaching. Diary writing can encourage you to be more selective, reflective and analytical than you would be if you were reporting verbally to a colleague or just thinking to yourself about a lesson. The process will help you to 'open windows' on your own teaching (see the activity *The Johari Window* in the first development circle for more on this). For these reasons, professional training courses sometimes use diary-type assignments as part of their syllabus and assessment procedures.

Writing a diary is an introspective and individual task. You may find this is a style of learning you feel more comfortable with than the more interpersonal and collaborative learning involved in other teacher development activities. If you derive *enjoyment* from keeping a personal diary you will probably enjoy keeping a teaching diary.

In terms of *recognition*, you can share your diary with colleagues and the ELT profession. There are several ways to do this:

- Circulating your e-journal.
- Informal discussion with colleagues.
- A formal report or presentation at a staff meeting.
- Publishing a blog. You can keep the ongoing diary online, inviting other teachers to read and comment as you go.
- Publishing the diary itself, or a report on what you have gained from using a diary, on an ELT website or teacher journal.

Keeping a teacher diary is not usually an *imposition*. You choose to do it. However it may be included by a school in a portfolio or teacher development scheme, or in a professional qualification.

# A teacher diary 2
## A step-by-step guide

### Rationale
You have committed to completing a teacher diary and looked at the range of options for formats. The aim of this guide is to help you set up and carry through the project, step by step.

### Activity
To organise your diary and manage the work involved, thinking about:
- what it will contain;
- how to organise it;
- a timeframe for your work, with deadlines and progress checks;
- what to do with it when it is finished.

### Step One
Decide your audience. Consider the four options in the 'My audience' table on page 86. Choose one, and think about the related questions.

### Step Two
Decide your contents. Will the diary have a focus? If so, what? In general, a focus which relates to what happens in the classroom, rather than the lesson planning stage, will be more appropriate. In the 'My focus' table are some examples of areas teachers often write about. The list, of course, is by no means exhaustive. Think about what worries or interests *you*.

### Step Three
Decide your timeframe and the number of groups you will write about. Make notes in the 'My timeframe' boxes, to help you decide which of the four models to choose. Think about your current teaching situation, particularly the most challenging elements.

### Step Four
Commit to the project. Based on your notes in Step Three, decide on a timetable and write it in the 'My timetable' grid.

### Step Five
Get started. Choose from the four options below how you will write your diary entries. You can experiment with different types of entry if you want.
- Narrative. 'Stream of consciousness'. (Write about what comes into your head.)
- Narrative. Focus on key moments. (Write about a specific incident or incidents in the lesson which you feel were significant.)
- Analytical. (Evaluate your lesson in terms of your focus.)
- A mixture of the above.

You will also need to consider when to write: soon after the lesson (hot) or after some time has elapsed (cool). Again, you can vary this from entry to entry.

### Step Six
Finish the diary. What happens now will depend on what you decided in Step One, although you may have changed your mind as the diary has developed. The diary can be:
- filed away;
- discussed with a colleague or friend;
- discussed with other teachers, reflecting on what you gained from the exercise;
- published.

### Step Seven
Celebrate! However you end, you will have made some important discoveries about your students and your teaching. Write down the most striking thing you have discovered.

### Stepping forward
Would you like to repeat this activity? If you found it valuable, you might want to make it a regular feature of your teacher development. You could decide to do a diary on a regular basis; once a year, for example, during a given month. If your first diary was private, you might want to go public next time, perhaps publishing it in a blog. Of course, you may have decided that diaries are not for you and concentrate on other development activities. This is also a good idea. It's up to you!

# A teacher diary 3

| Who will read the diary? | Points to consider | |
|---|---|---|
| Me | How will I motivate myself to do it? Will I let a friend read it? | |
| Me and other teachers | How will I organise the reading? Will I invite comments? How will I respond? Will a colleague and I keep diaries at the same time and read each other's? | |
| My supervisor on a course or DOS at my school | What are the agreed outcomes or assessment criteria? | |
| The profession | Who will publish it? Will it be raw entries or a diary study? If I opt for a study, who will do that part? | |

**My focus**

- giving instructions
- organising pair- and groupwork
- correcting errors
- my positioning in class
- use of the board

- my teacher talk
- dealing with pronunciation problems
- use of visual supports for learning
- use of movement in class
- student misbehaviour

- student attention
- student talk
- student participation
- use of learners' mother tongue
- use of teacher's mother tongue

**My timeframe**

| Intensive, with a single group<br>A short diary (eg 2 weeks) with a focus on one class | Slow burn, with a single group<br>A long diary (eg 2–6 months) with a focus on one class |
|---|---|
| Intensive, using various groups<br>A short diary (eg 2 weeks) with a focus on several or all my classes | Slow burn, using various groups<br>A long diary (eg 2–6 months) with a focus on several or all my classes |

**My timetable**

Start date: _____   Number of entries: _____

End date: _____   Entry dates: _____

# A teaching portfolio 1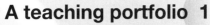
## A practical project

Richards and Farrell refer to two kinds of portfolio: *the working portfolio* and *the showcase portfolio*. The working portfolio is put together for primarily developmental purposes and will probably contain more critical reflection of your own work and even examples of failures. The showcase portfolio is aimed at 'presenting' yourself for a new job or promotion, and therefore is likely to reflect the highlights of your teaching career, 'a cleaned up version of my professional self', as David Nunan puts it. This is the kind of portfolio often used by freelance workers such as artists, designers and architects to demonstrate the range of their work to potential clients. A portfolio can be a mixture of working and showcase.

Here is a definition of a portfolio which refers to the *working portfolio*, with its emphasis on personal reflection and development:

> '*A professional portfolio is an evolving collection of carefully selected or composed professional thoughts, goals and experiences that are threaded with reflection and self-assessment. It represents who you are, what you do, why you do it, where you have been, where you are, where you want to go, and how you plan getting there.*'
> (Evans)

This second definition refers to the *showcase portfolio*, with an emphasis on the display and representation of your development and your ability to contribute to the profession:

> (A portfolio is …) '*a purposeful collection of any aspect of a teacher's work that tells the story of a teacher's effort, skills, abilities, achievements and contributions to his or her colleagues, institution, academic discipline or community.*'
> (Browne and Wolf-Quintero)

So we can think of a portfolio as:

- A story of your life as a teacher.
- A way of demonstrating your ongoing development.
- A CV fleshed out with examples.
- A tool for promoting your ongoing development.
- A record of your philosophy of teaching.
- A structured collection of materials you have made for teaching.

It places you as a teacher at the centre of your work. It allows you to view your work in terms of your personal achievements, though this, of course, will include your contribution to your school and other institutions.

A portfolio can take some time to complete. We can say 'complete' on the understanding that it is motivating to give a long-term developmental project a beginning and an end, even if you decide to repeat it soon afterwards or on a regular basis. This is what makes it special, memorable, rewarding and fun. If you make it ongoing it will become buried in routine, tiresome and unremarkable. Aim for a feature film, not a soap opera!

### What form can it take?
The form the portfolio takes will reflect your aims and what you want it to contain.

- It can be a big file containing examples on paper of your work, such as materials and course plans, as well as pictures, recordings and DVDs.
- It can be an electronic document which includes document files, PowerPoint presentations, DVD clips, audio files and links to web sites.
- It can be a webpage, MySpace or blog, including all the above, with added design features such as visuals and menus.

Electronic forms are preferable from an ecological point of view and more practical if you

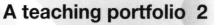

# A teaching portfolio 2
## A practical project

need to carry them around. A portfolio attached to a job CV works best as an attachment or webpage which the employer can open and browse at will. For a personal, developmental compilation, a paper-based file may be the best option. Bear in mind that some items, such as DVDs, tapes and certain materials, may not be easily stored electronically.

The portfolio can contain whatever you want it to contain. There are no rules. Your choice will depend on the type of portfolio you want to produce and your own interests. You can compile it *retro-spectively* or *pro-spectively*. In the former case, you sort out materials and activities you have already done and compile them (a bit like taking a pile of photos you have stuffed away in a drawer and collating them in a photo album). In the latter, you plan to do new activities or make new materials to include (like planning to take some more photos for your album). One way to make a portfolio is to select and then make a compilation of activities from *The Developing Teacher*.

### What can it contribute to your development?
We can look at the idea of portfolios in terms of the four motivations for development, captured in the acronym RISE.

In terms of **recognition**, if you are applying for a new post or promotion, a portfolio is likely to impress, particularly if it showcases your work in the classroom. In addition, a good portfolio may well be used as a model of best practice within a school and is likely to attract interest from other teachers. If you are a freelance teacher, your portfolio/website may be a key factor in attracting work.

A portfolio often is a compulsory element of Continuous Professional Development programmes in schools and institutions. If this is the case, the decision about whether to produce one has been made for you, an **imposition**. How it contributes to your development depends then on your attitude and how you put it together. As one teacher explained:

*'Completing a portfolio once a year seems like a chore each time it comes round, but I always end up finding the process of reflecting on my work useful and I am often pleasantly surprised to see how much I have achieved.'*

As far as **self-improvement** is concerned, the process of completing a portfolio will generate reflection on your work and give you a clearer understanding of your contribution to your students, your colleagues and your profession.

In the case of the *retro-spective* portfolio, the process of compiling involves reliving past experiences and seeing them from a new perspective. For example, you may decide to organise your jumble of favourite materials you have created in chronological order for your portfolio. This will help you to understand how your approach to teaching has changed over time. Both the process and the final product will reinforce this reflection.

In the case of the *pro-spective* portfolio, you may find yourself committing to new activities to fill perceived 'gaps'. For example, you decide to include a section on student feedback and then realise you have no examples to hand. This may lead you to getting some feedback from your students, perhaps using an activity suggested in *The Developing Teacher*.

Finally, provided you feel it is worthwhile, you will gain **enjoyment** from the process of working on the portfolio and experience a sense of satisfaction in the final product. As with the photo album, your emotional reactions, visualisations, remembering and reorganising will bring you pleasure and satisfaction, even if some of the photos you find may occasionally cause you to wince with regret or embarrassment!

# A teaching portfolio 3
## A step-by-step guide

### Rationale

Once you are committed to completing a portfolio, you need to consider how to go about putting it together. It can include material produced in the natural course of your work, as well as material or items produced specially for the portfolio. You can also include any of the activities from *The Developing Teacher*.

### Activity

To answer the following questions:
- What will the portfolio contain?
- How will I organise it?
- What is my timeframe for completing it?

### Step One

Think about what type of portfolio you want to produce and how you will present it. Tick the descriptions in the 'My portfolio' Pro-forma on page 90 which best apply, and add notes where appropriate. Discuss with a colleague.

### Step Two

Think about what will go in the portfolio. Look at the list of items in 'A portfolio checklist' on page 91 which could be incorporated, and tick the ones you intend to include. Spend some time discussing this with a colleague. Perhaps select a maximum of twelve.

### Step Three

Decide how you will organise the portfolio. On page 90 are four suggested ways of dividing it up. Discuss the pros and cons of each with a colleague and think of at least one other way of organising your portfolio. Choose one of the four, or choose your own.

### Step Four

Return to your list of contents from Step Two. Match the items to the appropriate section from your chosen format from Step Three. For example, if you have decided to include 'Reports on classes I have observed', this could fit in the section 'Teacher growth' of the CAST model. You now have a contents page for your portfolio, divided into sections.

### Step Five

Set deadlines. Copy your contents into a table format like the 'deadlines' example. List items with deadlines and notes. Spread out the deadlines. As a rule, allow a total of 4–12 weeks. If you go beyond three months, you may lose interest and focus. In some cases a portfolio may span an academic year (nine months). In this case, plan the whole nine months, giving yourself a monthly objective or objectives.

### Step Six

Once you have incorporated all the contents, put the finishing touches to the portfolio. This may include:
- a clear contents page;
- an attractive presentation of the materials;
- checking for accuracy.

Get a colleague to give you some feedback, and make adjustments accordingly.

### Step Seven

Congratulations! You have completed your portfolio. Celebrate.

### Stepping forward

Do a portfolio once a year, or alternate with a diary so you do one every two years. If you found it a very helpful experience, why not share it with others? You could do this by writing an article about it, giving a presentation to colleagues or at a conference. If you do this, concentrate on communicating *how* you chose to do it and *what* you got out of the experience. Don't dwell on the actual contents of the portfolio, as this is usually specific to you and of less interest to fellow teachers.

If you didn't find the activity rewarding in terms of your development, don't repeat it. Find something else to do instead, to move forward. The decision is yours.

# A teaching portfolio  4

## My portfolio

| | | |
|---|---|---|
| A showcase portfolio | | |
| A working portfolio | | |
| A CV fleshed out with examples | | |
| A demonstration of my ongoing development to an employer or potential clients | | |
| The story of my life as a teacher | | |
| Paper format | | |
| Electronic format | | |
| Mixed format | | |

## The organisation

| FIVE CIRCLES | CAST | TAP | 123 |
|---|---|---|---|
| 1 Me | 1 Contributions to the school and profession | 1 Teaching | 1 First job |
| 2 Me and my students | 2 Approach and philosophy | 2 Administration | 2 Second job |
| 3 Me and my colleagues | 3 Student growth | 3 Professional development | 3 Third job |
| 4 Me and my school | 4 Teacher growth | | |
| 5 Me and my profession | | | |

**YOUR OWN**

## The deadlines

| Item | Deadline | Notes |
|---|---|---|
| *Feedback from peers* | *14th March* | *Ask Juan, Nicola and Fiona for a paragraph.* |
| *DVD of me teaching* | *28th March* | *Find someone to operate camera (Chemi?), think about good extract to shoot. Can someone edit it? Ask Chemi.* |
| *Sample teaching materials* | *7th April* | *Sort through file and select three.* |

# A teaching portfolio 5

| A portfolio checklist | |
|---|---|
| Account of achievements of my students, such as passing exams, accessing university, getting a job | |
| Account of classroom research I have done | |
| Account of critical incidents and how I dealt with them | |
| Comments on mentoring I have done | |
| Comments on relationships with colleagues | |
| Copy of my qualifications | |
| Critique of my school's curriculum | |
| DVD of my teaching | |
| Examples of my students' work | |
| Feedback from bosses | |
| Feedback from a colleague/boss on observation of my classes | |
| Feedback from peers | |
| Formal feedback from students | |
| Informal peer support and guidance I have given and received | |
| Joint projects | |
| Diary entries | |
| Lesson plans | |
| List of books I have read which have influenced me, with an explanation | |
| List of courses I have taken | |
| List of groups I am a member of, with a description of the group activity | |
| List of journals I read regularly | |
| Notes and materials from conferences and workshops I have attended | |
| Notes of appreciation and cards from students | |
| Photos of me and my students in class | |
| Presentations to colleagues | |
| Professional development plan for myself | |
| Published articles, materials, book reviews | |
| Reports on classes I have observed | |
| Sample assessment procedures/material I use with my students | |
| Self-evaluations | |
| Special projects | |
| Statement of how I have developed over a given period of time | |
| Statement of my teaching philosophy | |
| Teaching materials I have prepared | |
| Workshops I have given | |
| Writing I have had published | |

# A teacher development scheme 1
## A professional project

When teacher development activities are organised and promoted within an institutional framework or educational community and systematically recorded in some way, we can refer to this as a scheme or programme. While the diary and portfolio projects fall more within the inner circles of the 'five circles' model, this type of activity corresponds to the outer circles, as it involves engaging with colleagues and probably the school where you work.

### What form can it take?
A teacher development scheme is like a teaching portfolio that is organised and supported by your colleagues and your school. As with the portfolio, it can include a selection of any of the activities described in *The Developing Teacher*, although the emphasis may be more on collaborative activities such as peer observation, self-observation, workshops and attendance at conferences. Whatever the *content* of a development scheme, there are important considerations for the *setting up*. Key features for success are:

- Ownership. If you are a participant in a scheme, you need to feel you are at the centre of the project. If you are leading the scheme, you need to help foster this.
- Incentive. Whether voluntary or compulsory, the scheme needs to have a clear idea of potential benefits. These could be intrinsic (a sense of personal achievement) and extrinsic (a prize).
- Uptake from influential group members. If respected and influential members of a group participate, others are likely to follow.
- Modelling and support from the person setting up the scheme. If this is you, make sure you participate and are seen to be committed to your own development as well as helping others with theirs.
- Follow-up, with scheduled checks on progress.
- Time limit. Nothing is more demotivating than the thought that this could go on forever. A maximum of three months? Remember: feature film, not soap opera.

### What can it contribute to your development?
We have noted Julian Edge's claim that *development* is something you do to yourself, as opposed to *training*, which other people do to you. If this is the case, the terms *teacher development scheme* or *teacher development programme* appear somewhat contradictory. If I am doing my own developing, how do schemes and programmes fit in? If they are imposed, in what way can they be developmental? However, many schools and teachers themselves support the idea that teacher development is something which can be actively sponsored and promoted by teacher groups, schools and institutions in the interests of all concerned. There are various potential participants or stakeholders in a development scheme.

You may find yourself in one or more of these roles: participating teacher, organising teacher, director of studies, or school owner or director. What you get out of the scheme in terms of your personal professional development will depend on the role you play.

From the point of view of an educational community, participation in a teacher development scheme may be part of a formal appraisal, a job requirement or a voluntary activity organised by the school or by teachers themselves to promote development. Both 'top-down' and 'bottom-up' style schemes can be equally effective vehicles for development when participants are totally committed to them.

All four RISE motivations (Recognition, Imposition, Self-improvement and Enjoyment) may come into play, then, when engaging in a teacher development scheme. Teacher attitudes towards such schemes, and the amount of development which happens, will vary according to the scenario, the teachers themselves and the leadership from the school or the person in charge of the project.

# A teacher development scheme 2
## A step-by-step guide

### Rationale
Setting up a development scheme in a school is a tremendous challenge, but the rewards of a successful scheme can be substantial for you and your school. The 'costs', particularly in terms of people's time, can be high, so the benefits need to be assessed carefully. This activity is for both teachers and directors of studies who wish to set up a teacher development programme.

### Activity
To set up a teacher development scheme.

### Step One
Do some reflection, before you start. Make notes, using the Pro-forma 'Considerations for teachers and schools' on page 94, with a colleague if possible.

### Step Two
Do some research. Sound out two members of staff separately and informally, one you think will be keen and one not so keen. Explain the idea of the scheme, hint at possible contents or procedures, the work involved. After the conversations, add to your notes from Step One.

### Step Three
Invite teachers to a meeting. Before the meeting, review the 'Six points for successful schemes' checklist. Does your scheme have these? Specify how in the right-hand column.

### Step Four
In the meeting, present your ideas, aiming to cover the six areas from Step Three as well as you can. Here are some tips for the meeting:
- Let teachers choose what goes in the scheme from a list of options. The activities in *The Developing Teacher* are all suitable for inclusion in a scheme of this kind. Teachers can agree which activities to incorporate, perhaps using a pyramid discussion.
- The choice of activities may be limited by constraints. Peer observation, for example, may have logistic and financial implications. Make any constraints clear to teachers.
- Be enthusiastic about the benefits and honest about the costs.
- Commit to participating in the scheme yourself.
- Make it clear if the scheme is compulsory or voluntary.
- Set a date for a round-up/feedback meeting (see Step Seven).

### Step Five
At the end of the meeting, come to an agreement about what the scheme will contain and a timeframe. You can use the activity *SMARTER planning* in circle four to help you do this. Each teacher completes a table like the 'Schedule' example on page 94.

### Step Six
Plan a regular time to meet or e-mail, to report on progress and encourage and support each other. This could be weekly or monthly, depending on the schedule you have decided. Divide the teachers into sub-groups, if necessary, with a group leader. The maximum group size for these meetings should be six, to ensure effective participation. In these meetings or reports, teachers can:
- 'show and tell' what they have achieved;
- request help and advice from colleagues;
- encourage each other and give maximum support.

### Step Seven
Hold your round-up/feedback meeting. This is for teachers to:
- talk about what they have gained from the scheme;
- make suggestions on how it can be improved;
- celebrate the completion of the scheme with champagne or cake and coffee.

### Stepping forward
Think about how successful the scheme was. You should have a good idea after Step Seven, but if you are still not sure, get some more individual feedback from the participants. If it wasn't a success, this could be because you didn't set it up well or because it just isn't the best way forward for you and your colleagues. If the scheme was a success and you want to repeat it, suggest that someone else organises it next time. Step back and let someone else step forward!

# A teacher development scheme 3

## Considerations for teachers and schools

What do I gain as a teacher from the scheme? (More teaching skills or knowledge? Improved relationships with colleagues? Enjoyment?)

What will the school gain from this scheme? (Better quality teaching? More students? Staff loyalty?)

Is the scheme compulsory or optional? What sanctions or incentives are there? Are these explicit or implicit?

What support do teachers need? (Files, worksheets, help with videoing classes, advice, time off teaching for peer observation, financial help with training or attending conferences?)

How much time am I prepared to allocate to the scheme?

What would happen if I didn't set up/participate in the scheme? Are there alternative ways to meet the aims set out in the first two boxes?

## Six points for successful schemes

| | | |
|---|---|---|
| 1 | Ownership | |
| 2 | Incentive | |
| 3 | Uptake | |
| 4 | Modelling/support | |
| 5 | Follow-up | |
| 6 | Time limit | |

## Schedule

| What? | When by? | Notes |
|---|---|---|
| *Observe two colleagues.* | *Feb 28th* | *Arrange time to observe Sonja and Ana. Check if they want me to observe for anything in particular. Pro-forma?* |
| *Get feedback from class X.* | *Feb 14th* | *Use a feedback activity from the Foord book.* |
| *Write a book review for colleagues.* | *March 14th* | *New book on pronunciation activities in staffroom?* |

# From the editors

One of the main premises of *The Developing Teacher* is that teachers themselves are the most powerful agents of change and development in their own professional career. Duncan Foord has written a book that is innovative in that it provides practical, achievable, accessible and enjoyable activities for teachers to shape their own development.

- An examination of different aspects of, and issues in, teacher development.
- A discussion of how teachers learn and what prevents them from learning.
- A survey of the literature on language teacher development, helpful for those studying MA or Diploma courses on the subject.
- A model for teacher development which is both comprehensive and user-friendly.

- Circles of expanding development, embracing all aspects of the language teacher's life, from students and colleagues to schools and the profession at large.
- Activities that teachers can start doing right away and which take little time.
- Procedures that follow a step-by-step outline, making them easy to understand at a glance – perfect for the busy teacher.
- Tasks, checklists and questionnaires that promote reflective practice and encourage commitment.

- A view of further teacher development.
- Longer-term projects – a diary, a portfolio and a teacher development programme.
- Step-by-step guides to each project, enabling and empowering teachers to commit to their continuing development.

In short, *The Developing Teacher* aims to be a comprehensive manual that is an ideal vehicle for teachers who wish to take control of their own development: but also for those people in positions of responsibility for teacher development: directors of studies or administrators. It can also be seen as a useful complement to courses in language teacher education.

We hope we have been successful in helping to communicate Duncan's knowledge and experience, and his commitment to the profession, and that you find the book as useful as the editors and the author found it exciting to put together.

**Mike Burghall**
**Lindsay Clandfield**

# From the publishers

D E L T A   T E A C H E R   D E V E L O P M E N T   S E R I E S

A pioneering new series of books for English Language Teachers
with professional development in mind.

**The Developing Teacher**
by Duncan Foord
ISBN 978-1-905085-22-44

**Teaching Unplugged**
by Luke Meddings and Scott Thornbury
ISBN 978-1-905085-19-4

For details of future titles in the series, please contact the publisher or visit
the DTDS website at www.deltapublishing.co.uk/DTDS

---

Also from DELTA PUBLISHING

*professional perspectives*

A series of practical methodology books designed to provide teachers of English
with fresh insights, innovative ideas and original classroom materials.

**Creating Conversation in Class**
by Chris Sion
ISBN 978-0-953309-88-7

**Talking Business in Class**
by Chris Sion
ISBN 978-1-900783-64-4

**Challenging Children**
by Henk van Oort
ISBN 978-1-900783-93-4

**The MINIMAX Teacher**
by Jon Taylor
ISBN 978-0953309-89-4

**Dealing with Difficulties**
by Luke Prodromou and Lindsay Clandfield
ISBN 978-1-905085-00-2

**The Resourceful English Teacher**
by Jonathan Chandler and Mark Stone
ISBN 978-0-953309-81-8

**Humanising your Coursebook**
by Mario Rinvolucri
ISBN 978-0-954198-60-2

**Unlocking Self-expression through NLP**
by Judith Baker and Mario Rinvolucri
ISBN 978-1-900783-88-0

**Spontaneous Speaking**
by David Heathfield
ISBN 978-1-900783-92-7

**Using the Mother Tongue**
by Sheelagh Dellar and Mario Rinvolucri
ISBN 978-0-954198-61-9

Please contact the publisher for further details:
*Tel* +44 (0)1306 731770   *E-mail* info@deltapublishing.co.uk
*Web* www.deltapublishing.co.uk

---